Building Independent Readers

With Interactive Read-Alouds & Shared Reading

Valorie Falco
& Rochelle P. Soloway

New York • Toronto • London • Auckland • Sydney
Mexico City • New Delhi • Hong Kong • Buenos Aires

Cover design by Brian LaRossa
Interior design by Teresa B. Southwell
Interior photographs by Valorie Falco and Teresa Kaplan
Editor: Joanna Davis-Swing
Copy Editor: Chris Borris
ISBN: 978-0-545-22755-1
Copyright © 2011 Valorie Falco and Rochelle P. Soloway
All rights reserved.
Printed in the U.S.A.

2 3 4 5 6 7 8 9 10   40   17 16 15 14 13 12 11

Contents

Acknowledgments

When we envision all the people who have helped us, directly or indirectly, write this book it is easy to see a tapestry, woven together with old threads and new threads. It is in the weaving that these threads come together in a rich and lively way. The first threads that stand out belong to all the authors and presenters who have inspired us over the years. As we read and listened to Ellin Keene, Stephanie Harvey, Franki Sibberson, Debbie Miller, Jeff Wilhelm, Linda Hoyt, Donna Scanlon, Irene Fountas and Gay Su Pinnell, Regie Routman, Diane Snowball, Lucy Caulkins, Shelley Harwayne, Isoke Nia, Ralph Fletcher, and Georgia Heard, we rethought what we believed about teaching reading.

Our colleagues over the years have provided the most supportive threads. For Val, Ginny Mondshein, Christine Schade, Diane McNiven, Mignonne Philips, Kathy Bartley, Grace Bennett, Amy Klugman, Gina Baldwin, Dianna Reagan, Betsy Smith, Chris Porter, Betsy Malloy, and Jean O'Donnell have been her go-to people. To work alongside these master teachers and administrators has been an honor. They have been supportive, understanding, and willing to give her a push when she has needed it.

For Rochelle, Susan McDonald, Alicia Rizzo, Linda Sauer, Dianne Clarke, Lyn Clark, Julie Grec, Bob Walton, Bill Wendell, Susan London, and Karen Cloutier were the teaching colleagues, co-learners, and educators to whom she could talk literacy endlessly: They never said, "Let's change the subject!"

More threads for Rochelle were all the great teachers, principals, and superintendents who allowed her to come and work with them and their students. It is absolutely true that Rochelle has learned far more than she could ever impart. A special group of colleagues with whom she worked in those schools and districts, Judy Dutton, Lisa Henkel, Karen Conroy, Michelle Whiting, and Stella Ritter, helped her think through many things in this book.

A thread that brought so many books into Val's life is the one belonging to Frank Hodge of Hodge Podge Books. Frank always knew that reading aloud to our students was one of the best gifts we could give them.

A long thread of Val's is the one associated with the Bethlehem Central School District. Over the years, Val has worn many hats in the district: teacher, language arts coordinator, and staff developer, and in each role there were leaders who supported and inspired her, including: Briggs McAndrews, Don Robillard, Heidi Bonacquist, Dorothy McDonald, Mike Tebbano, and her current principal, Laura Heffernan.

Rochelle's professional threads began in Australia, at schools like her last school, Ranfurly Elementary School, where she was the curriculum and literacy coordinator, kindergarten teacher, and primary grade coordinator. The threads continued as she finished her career in Australia as a curriculum project officer, responsible for curriculum development in 44 elementary, middle, and high schools in a rural area.

Rochelle's threads then wove their way for miles and miles arriving first in New York City and then in Albany. These first American threads were part of the AUSSIE and Mondo Publishing staff development sections—especially important, those of Diane Snowball and Mark Vineis. The later threads brought Capital Region BOCES and Questar into Rochelle's tapestry. These settings were full of wonderful colleagues and leaders who trusted in her ability to help schools and teachers with literacy. This part of the tapestry is made strong by Gladys Cruz at Questar and Mary Capobianco at Capital Region BOCES.

Our weaving came together when we were staff developers at the Literacy Center. These threads were made vibrant from the work we did with our friend Liz Pascuzzi, who taught us so much about early literacy. We spent hours talking, reading, researching, and coming up with a way to put it all together for the teachers with whom we were working.

Over the last year, two threads have stood out, those of friends and colleagues, Grace Bennett and Jean O'Donnell, who read and reread every chapter. Our writing and thinking flows better due to Jean's purple editing pen and all the hard questions both asked.

All the children we've taught over the years are evident in this tapestry. Most recently, Val had the joy of having most of the same students for two years, first as second graders and then as third graders. Many lessons were modeled with these students and they taught us a lot. A thread that has stood out in Val's classroom belongs to Teresa Kaplan, her classroom aide and friend. Every classroom should have a Mrs. Kaplan.

The threads that anchor not just this tapestry but our lives are those of our friends and families. Our friends celebrated so many moments associated with this book. They provided dinners, wine, and the much-needed chocolate.

Val's friends' threads show Bert, Lois, Molly, Monica, Chris G., Sarah, Marilyn, Sandy, Beth, and Susan and her sister Jaye. This special group of women has provided so much with their words of encouragement, their joy in her accomplishments, and their help with the practical things in life, like picking up her children, feeding her family, and making sure she had some great clothes.

Val's husband, George, and her daughters, Molly and Madeline, have never wavered in their support. They didn't complain when she said, "Rochelle and I need to go away for the weekend to write," and they celebrated each completed chapter. George has believed in this project from the start, and Val is so grateful for his love and encouragement.

Rochelle's family has provided her strongest thread. Her husband, Ron, was ever patient and supportive, as were her children, Samantha, Liam, Gemma, and Hannah. They may not know much about teaching reading but they continually demonstrate their belief in Rochelle's work. Of course, Rochelle's mum, Joy Robinson, is by far her best advocate in the world. Joy's unwavering support, "Of course, yes, you can write a book," made it possible.

The tapestry comes together with the skillful hands of our editors at Scholastic, Joanna Davis-Swing and Sarah Glasscock. Joanna guided us through the process, valuing our beliefs while pushing us to find a structure that was both engaging and informative. Her questions challenged us to think deeply and to clarify our thinking so our lessons and understanding of interactive read-alouds and shared reading were accessible to new and experienced teachers alike. Sarah's editing, comments, and questions helped us through the revision process. Her ability to point out kindly where the writing needed to be "massaged" helped us as writers and educators.

We are so thankful for all the threads and the way they have all come together to bring this book to fruition.

Introduction

One Friday, after a particularly frustrating week, we were sitting at a coffee shop talking about the conferences we were having with our students. At the time, Rochelle was a literacy coach working with fourth graders, and Valorie was teaching second grade. We noticed that rather than conversing about what they were reading, our students repeatedly waited for us to ask questions about the book they were reading and were happy to give us very literal responses often drawn from the cover or the last section they'd read. As our questions became more inferential, even many of our "best" readers gave us the "deer in the headlights" look. We were modeling lessons with interactive read-alouds. We were using wonderful short texts for shared reading, but many of our students were not independently using the strategies and skills we were teaching in these lessons. Why?

That question made us do some serious reflecting on our teaching. At about that time, Rochelle attended a conference with Jeff Wilhelm. As he talked about his gradual release of responsibility for learning model, Rochelle had that "aha!" moment. We were releasing the responsibility to our students too soon. Our lessons were good, but there was another step in Wilhelm's gradual release model that we had often neglected—the movement from demonstration to shared demonstration before expecting our students to undertake independent practice. The independent practice part, the real long-term learning that is not lost in a week or two, where the strategy doesn't need constant reteaching, was what we hoped to achieve, but we weren't getting to that point with enough of our students.

At about this same time, we were inspired by the work of Ellin Keene on essential literacy. Her ideas made us look more closely at whole-group, small-group, and independent work. How could we maximize our teaching with each configuration?

Ellin's work, along with the work of Linda Hoyt, Stephanie Harvey, and Tony Stead, made us examine the kinds of texts we were using with our students. We were using a lot of fiction but very little nonfiction. How could our students comprehend nonfiction when we only touched on its text structures and features briefly?

This book is the result of our careful consideration of these questions and the teaching we did to move our students toward independence. We have tried to be very honest about the lessons that worked and those that didn't. We aren't presenting a series of scripted lessons, but rather lessons that show our thinking and modeling over time.

In the process of writing Chapter 3, we were required to look closely at genres. What we assumed to be pretty straightforward turned out to be much more complicated than we ever anticipated. For us, it became clear that what we were really talking about when we said we were studying mysteries or fantasy was text type, not genre. It might seem like a small detail, but our language should make it easier for our students, not harder. Certainly, when we say text type, it is easy to explain to our students that a certain text is a type of text and then explain its characteristics.

In fact, each of the six chapters in this book sent us on a journey to make our thinking as clear as it could be. In the midst of this journey, we were constantly doing interactive read-alouds and shared reading with our students. More than once, the research led us in one direction, but our students led us in another.

Each chapter follows a consistent pattern. We usually start with a lesson detailing the type of teaching discussed in the chapter. We like to mix practice and theory as often as possible. Theory can be dry, but we both rely on it to anchor our teaching and student learning. We hope you find the mixture of practice and explanation satisfying to read and useful in your teaching practice.

Chapter 1

Teaching Strategies and Releasing Responsibility: The Foundational Role of Interactive Read-Alouds and Shared Reading

Welcome to Val's Classroom

As Val's second graders gather on the rug in front of her, she holds up the book *Amazing Bats* by Seymour Simon. Val shares with students that when she begins reading a nonfiction book, she needs to first think about what she knows about the topic, activating her schema, or background knowledge, so she can better comprehend the text.

She tells students, "When I look at this book, I immediately think about the time we had a bat in our house. I knew it was a lot smaller than I was, but I was scared and I sure didn't like it flying around my room. I also think about the myth that bats will fly into your hair. Even though I know this isn't true, I still worry a bit about that when I see them flying around at dusk in the summer. As I am worrying, I always remind myself that bats eat mosquitoes, so I'm glad they're around. All this thinking goes on before I even open the book. Now, when I start to read the book, I am ready to learn more about bats. I can add to what I already know about bats, or I can change my thinking if what I am thinking is not quite right."

Thus begins Val's interactive read-aloud on activating our schema before we read. As she proceeds, she will share her thinking of how her schema affects her reading of this text, emphasizing how her thinking is either confirmed or changed as she reads.

Why did Val teach this lesson?

Val did an interactive read-aloud with her class as part of her whole-group instruction on schema. We know effective reading instruction for grades 2 through 5 must include whole-group, small-group, independent reading, and individual conferences—but how does a teacher find the time to do it all? We place our whole-group instruction at the beginning of the daily reading block, scaffolding skills and strategies that all students need and creating common language to interact with text, thus establishing a powerful forum for instruction. Within this whole-group instructional time, which usually takes about 15 to 20 minutes, we place our interactive read-alouds and shared reading.

The Essentials of Creating a Mental Map for Reading Instruction

The one thing that every successful teacher of reading needs is a mental map or organizer of how the different processes of reading fit together to create comprehension. Although many people have taught us many things, for the purposes of this book, we are going to explore the mental map that has stuck with us. We rely on it to help us make instructional decisions in our teaching of reading.

Where did our mental map begin?

During the many years that we have been teaching, we have both been inspired by the many speakers we have had the privilege of hearing. These people, at the forefront of the reading field, have educated us to do better and try harder to help every student develop his or her reading potential. It is critical to read or listen to educators who have researched, and can explain, the complicated processes that shape reading behavior. We know so much more now than we ever did about reading instruction, and it is important to use this new knowledge to better our teaching.

Our map starts with the work of Ellin Oliver Keene in *To Understand: New Horizons in Reading Comprehension* (2008). After many years of research and study in the field, she classified six systems in reading: three surface structure systems and three deeper surface systems.

The surface structures—*grapho-phonic, lexical, syntactic*— include decoding, learning high-frequency words, building instant recognition of words, reading fluently, gaining literal understanding, recognizing text structures and genre, and so on, are much easier to teach and to assess, and so many times in our careers, we have concentrated on teaching them. While these surface structures are vitally important, the deep structures are what proficient readers use to construct a deeper and enduring meaning from a text. These structures—*semantic, schematic,* and *pragmatic*—are thinking processes that include precise word usage, accessing prior knowledge, and reading for purpose and audience. Since these processes are invisible, they are much harder for teachers to instruct and assess. In the past, these deeper structures were neglected during reading instruction, especially in the younger grades.

Ellin Keene says that teachers in the primary grades need to put about 50 percent of their instructional time into the surface structures and about 50 percent into the deep structures. We agree. We know that surface structures are especially important as children begin to read and develop the bank of words, phrases, and sentence structures that they instantly recognize to start the journey toward being proficient readers. However, instructional time does need to be put into the deep structures so that students are orchestrating all systems in order to comprehend from the beginning. This allows early readers to understand what it means to be a reader. If they only concentrate on the surface structures, reading becomes merely a decoding and memorization activity. As students progress in their reading behaviors and text levels, traditionally in grades 2 through 5, much more time needs to be devoted to these deep systems, building up to about 80 percent in grades 4 and 5.

For transitional readers in grades 2 and 3, interactive read-alouds and shared reading provide excellent opportunities to develop reading behaviors to activate the deep structures. Teachers read the text aloud, thus taking over the work of the surface structures (decoding). This allows students time to learn about the increasing complexity of semantic, schematic, and pragmatic strategies.

But semantic, schematic, and pragmatic are technical terms, and when we stand in front of our classes each morning, what do these terms mean? Many teachers have relied on Ellin Keene, Stephanie Harvey, Ann Goudvis, and Debbie Miller to help with the translation. Again, the language for comprehension strategies that we are using comes from Ellin Keene's workshop that we attended in the fall of 2004.

These comprehension strategies are:

* Monitoring for meaning
* Determining importance
* Evoking mental images
* Synthesizing
* Relating new to known (schema)
* Questioning
* Inferring

In the current reading literature, there are slight differences in the terminology that authors use to name comprehension strategies. This is not a problem as long as you are comfortable with the terminology your school or district has chosen. We've created a chart showing the terms that different authors use: The chart compares the terms Keene, Harvey and Goudvis, Miller, and Fountas and Pinnell use in their texts. It can be a revelation to see the different terms that refer to the same strategy (see the Comprehension Strategy Terminology Chart in the Appendix, p. 114).

How did we use all this thinking to create our own mental maps?

After thinking about Keene's work, and what we knew about effective reading instruction, we set out to find a way to show teachers how this came together for us. The chart in Figure 1.2 on the next page is a result of our thinking.

This model divides our reading instruction into four quadrants. The center oval indicates the primary focus of the quadrants. The model also details the type of texts, the grouping size, and the cognitive strategies we teach within each of these components. Of course, the role of the teacher is to balance these components in ways that meet the needs of their students. We don't necessarily divide our time equally into four segments, but we do make decisions about which small-group context we use and how often. We use literature discussions primarily to study novels and generally use shorter texts in guided reading. For this book, we are talking about the second and third quadrants, which are highlighted (see Figure 1.3 on page 14).

Figure 1.2   Gradual Release of Responsibility in Reading

Independent:
You Do.
I Watch.

Demonstration:
I Do.
You Watch.

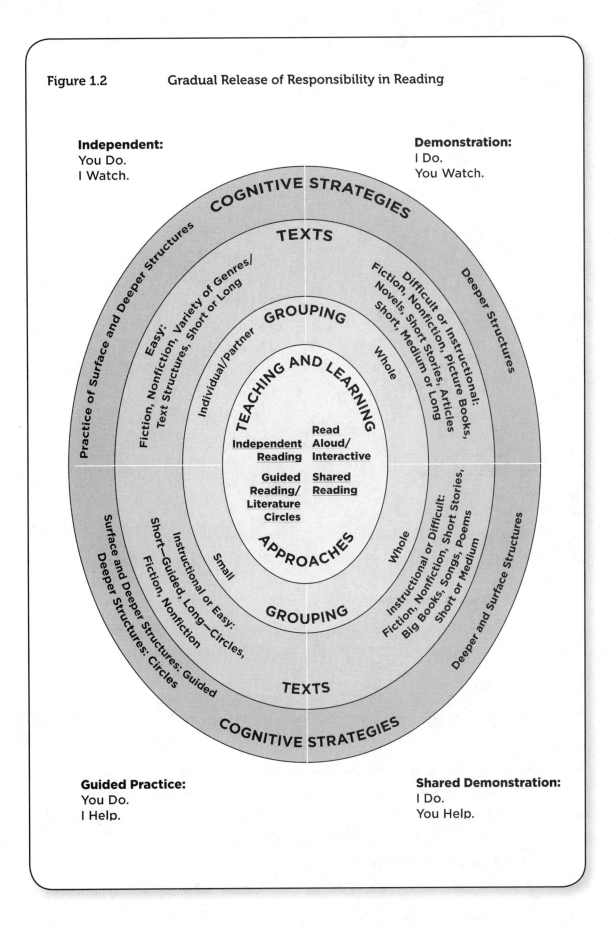

Guided Practice:
You Do.
I Help.

Shared Demonstration:
I Do.
You Help.

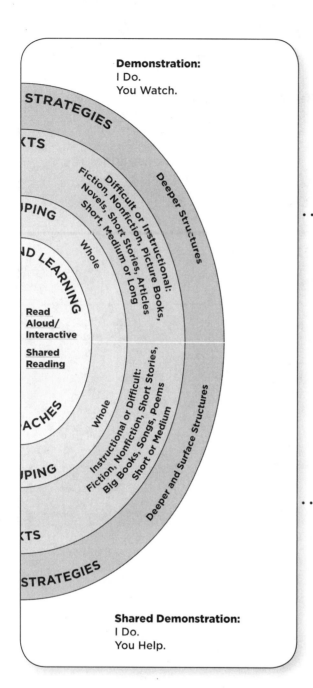

Demonstration:
I Do.
You Watch.

STRATEGIES

XTS

JPING

ND LEARNING

Read
Aloud/
Interactive

Shared
Reading

ACHES

JPING

XTS

STRATEGIES

Difficult or Instructional:
Fiction, Nonfiction, Picture Books,
Novels, Short Stories, Articles
Short, Medium or Long

Whole

Deeper Structures

Instructional or Difficult:
Fiction, Nonfiction, Short Stories,
Big Books, Songs, Poems
Short or Medium

Whole

Deeper and Surface Structures

Shared Demonstration:
I Do.
You Help.

Figure 1.3

Interactive read-alouds and shared reading appear in two quadrants, but for our reading map, they act as the anchor for the other quadrants. These two whole-class instructional methods help us build the foundation for most of the skills and strategies that children in grades 2–5 need to become proficient readers.

Interactive Read-Alouds:
Modeling Reading Strategies With the Whole Class

Interactive read-alouds as we define them, also called think-alouds by Stephanie Harvey (2000), focus on the teaching of strategies, structures, and genres within the context of the story. While the story or information is important, we enter the interactive read-aloud with a specific focus on a reading strategy. With short, explicit lessons, we can expose all our students to our thinking processes and invite them to practice using a strategy or understanding a structure or genre before they ever tackle it independently.

Modeling is a key feature of an interactive read-aloud. A teacher explicitly models her thinking by talking about it as she reads a text to her students. The text might be a picture book, a short story, an article from a magazine or a newspaper, a poem, or a letter. The teacher has decided on a specific strategy, structure, skill, or genre on which to focus. Her thinking aloud will make "visible" the process she is using to comprehend the text.

During an interactive read-aloud, the teacher is reading the text to students. Students do not have a copy; they do not need to be able to see the text, but they should be able to see the illustrations. They are watching and listening to the teacher read and making meaning of the text. As shown in Figure 1.4, Jeff Wilhelm (2001) refers to this step in the gradual release of responsibility as "I Do, You Watch." Since the teacher is in control of the text, it does not need to be a text that students are able to read independently.

Figure 1.4

Jeffrey D. Wilhelm's Gradual Release of Responsibility Model

I Do. You Watch.	I Do. You Help.	You Do. I Help.	You Do. I Watch.
Demonstration	Shared Demonstration	Guided Practice	Independent Practice

Interactive read-alouds can be used to introduce a new strategy, structure, skill, or genre to students, so finding a text that you like and that will be engaging to students is important. We've tried using texts that are highly recommended but that we personally don't enjoy, and the modeling with these texts seems flat. If we're not that interested, it's hard to keep our students interested. When we use a text that has hooked us, it is much easier to hook our students. They become interested in the text due to our enthusiasm, and then we begin to model the process we are using to read and comprehend the text. The specific language we use is the first vital step in helping our students understand our thinking.

How do you actually make the reading process visible?

 Let's return to Val's room . . .

After reading the first page of *Amazing Bats* by Seymour Simon, Val says, "Looking at this picture of the bat doesn't really make me like bats any better, but I am amazed at the way its wings look close up. I'm also wondering what kind of bat this is since it looks very different from the one we had in our house. I knew bats were mammals, but I didn't know that the scientific name for bats means 'hand-wing.'" Then Val comments that the text of this book is easy for her to read, but that it has information she didn't know. In fact, the pictures are helping her better understand the text.

Several pages later Val stops and comments, "Reading this book is not only adding to and changing my schema for bats, but it is also changing the way I think about informative texts. I never really thought about it, but I am realizing that if I don't have much schema, or understanding, about a topic, it is helpful to read easier books. This helps me build my schema so I can then tackle more complex books on the topic."

Val continues reading the book, stopping to point out how her schema is changing and how important that is to her understanding of what she is reading. This is especially true for reading nonfiction.

The students in Val's classroom are a community of learners, and in this lesson, they watch and listen to her thinking. Over the next few days, Val will invite students to join her in interacting with the text, thus allowing them to practice the strategy. Tomorrow, before reading *Killer Whales* (Simon, 2002), Val will talk to her students about how to participate in a discussion of an interactive read-aloud.

How will Val involve her students in the interactive read-aloud?

The next day, as students gather on the rug, Val says, "Throughout the year, we will explore different strategies for understanding a text. There will be times when I am sharing my thinking with you, times when you will be sharing your thinking with a partner, and times when you will be sharing your thinking with all of us. It will be important for all of us to listen to what others are saying about the text. It will help us have a deeper understanding of the text and ourselves as readers. Yesterday, you watched and listened as I read *Amazing Bats*. Today, we will interact together with this book, *Killer Whales* by Seymour Simon. We will see what we know about killer whales before we start reading. As we read, we will look to confirm or change our thinking." Before she starts reading, Val asks students to turn and talk with a partner about what they know about killer whales.

Turn and Talk

Turn and talk is one of the first procedures we teach our students. They choose a talk partner or have one selected for them. When prompted by the teacher, partners turn, knee to knee, eye to eye, and discuss the question or topic.

Two pairs of students engaged in a turn and talk

Then Val calls the class together again. "I heard a lot of you saying things like 'Killer whales are cool' or 'They are awesome' so I know you are interested in this topic. Did any of you share with your partner a fact you thought you knew about killer whales?"

- They are the largest whales.
- They are dangerous
- They attack people.
- They eat other fish.

Val charted the facts that children volunteered about whales.

Several children share the facts they know with the class.

As Val gets ready to read the book, she says, "Before I read this book, I had some ideas about whales that I learned weren't true, and I learned a lot of new and interesting facts. As I read, I will show you where my thinking has changed. I want you to listen for information that confirms what you have been thinking and information that changes your thinking."

After reading the first two pages of the book, Val stops and comments, "Right here in the first two pages I had to change my thinking about killer whales. Because they are so big, I assumed that they would move slowly, but now I know they are as fast as sharks."

After reading the next page, Val stops again and asks students if she has read anything that has confirmed or changed their thinking. Many students raise their hands. All are ready to share that the information on the chart is wrong: Killer whales don't attack people. Several point out that they confirmed the fact that killer whales eat fish. One child says, "But we have to add to the fact about eating fish because they also eat seals and penguins."

Val continues to read the book to the class, and together they discuss how their thinking has been confirmed or changed. At the end of the lesson, Val states, "As readers, we need to think about what we know about a topic before we begin to read. Then, when we are reading, we want to notice those 'aha! moments' when we confirm our ideas and those times when we have to have to change our thinking because we have new information."

> ### Do you do this intensive interaction with the text every time you read aloud to your students?

No, this would be too much; we do this explicit teaching, which we call interactive read-aloud, generally twice a week. We read to our students every day. These daily read-alouds are selected for their power as stories or informational texts to engage our students and for their enjoyment. Although the daily read-aloud might be a picture book or short text, it is more common for us to read a chapter book at this time. The discussion about these read-alouds is open-ended and most often about the story itself. There is enormous power in the language and conversations that grow out of this read-aloud time. This is also the time when we hope students will fall in love with the book and start or continue their journey as lifelong readers.

Releasing Responsibility With Shared Reading

 ### Let's Visit a Fifth-Grade Class With Rochelle

In her role as a literacy coach, Rochelle enters a fifth-grade classroom that has been learning about activating schema when students may have little or no schema for a topic or an idea. The teacher has introduced the strategy with the book *Faithful Elephants: A True Story of Animals, People, and War* (Tsuchiya, 1997) and then engaged students to practice the strategy with her with *Henry's Freedom Box* (Levine, 2007). She chose both of these books because she was certain her students had very little, if any, schema for the topics of these books. She knew she had to help her students develop strategies for building their schema when they faced a topic with which they were unfamiliar. The teacher now feels that her students are beginning to understand how to think about topics that they don't already know a lot about. They are ready to share the responsibility of reading the text and beginning to share the construction of its meaning.

The teacher has created an inviting space on a rug, and Rochelle will need to convince students to come and sit together in this space. Although they are reluctant to sit on the rug, Rochelle knows her lesson will have more engagement and power if she can gather this group together. The community feeling that can be built by students and teachers working collaboratively to understand a text is an essential part of shared reading.

As the class has been thinking about schema related to books with historical themes, Rochelle has decided to work on activating their schema with a different topic that moves away from the area of social studies. It is important for students to realize that they need to practice a strategy with different subject matters and genres. Rochelle assumes that students wouldn't have much schema for maggots, and especially for the topic of using maggots in hospitals. Rochelle chooses to share the text on maggots on an overhead projector.

She begins her lesson by saying, "You have been working on activating your schema, or background knowledge, when the topic is not one you know a lot about. Let's review the behaviors that you used to help you understand *Faithful Elephants* and *Henry's Freedom Box*." Students mention studying the title, cover, and blurb carefully before they start reading, reading more slowly, rereading sections to achieve more understanding, and using the illustrations to add to their knowledge of the events in the stories. Rochelle nods in agreement and continues, "Today, I'm going to ask you to think about an article whose topic I'm sure you won't have read much about. We won't be able to use a cover or blurb because this is an article, but we can use the other behaviors you mentioned: thinking about the title, rereading, and reading more slowly."

As Rochelle displays the text, "Gross but Good" from *Oh, Yuck! The Encyclopedia of Everything Nasty* (Masoff, 2000), on the overhead projector, students' interest levels rise. Rochelle begins by saying, "I'm going to read this article titled 'Gross but Good,' which is about maggots." At this point, several students groan in disgust, while several others say, "Cool!"

Rochelle asks, "Does anyone know anything about maggots?" One boy raises his hand and describes maggots in detail. It turns out that he has recently seen a television show on maggots. This is certainly not what Rochelle expected to happen, but it serves her purpose—engaging students in this text.

She confirms that the information is correct and goes on to say, "Most of what you told us was definitely gross. Now you all have some background for the 'gross' part of the article, but are you wondering about the 'good' things that maggots can do?"

Rochelle has only read the first two sentences when it's obvious that students are engaged with the text. She stops and asks students if they have any idea what the author has done to make everyone want to read more of this text. They indicate that the lead, with its descriptive language, hooked them. Rochelle continues with her reading.

By the time she has read the entire text aloud, students are fascinated with the idea that maggots are sometimes used in hospitals to eat decaying flesh from a wound. Of course, had she used a complex textbook and had students following along with her for a long period of time, the lesson would have fallen flat very quickly. We think this is why many teachers find managing shared reading difficult. On the other hand, when we use texts that grab students' attention, we are able to keep them engaged in the process of making meaning and comprehending a text.

What exactly is shared reading?

Shared reading can be a very powerful teaching approach that is versatile enough to be used during reading and content subjects. Several essential elements add to its power.

❖ **The text is short.**

It could be a short story, article, excerpt from a longer text, poem, or cartoon.

❖ **The text must be visible to all students as well as the teacher.**

This is one condition that makes shared reading different from a read-aloud or an interactive read-aloud. You can enlarge the text by using an electronic camera or overhead projector, charts, big books, and whiteboards. The fact that everyone can read the text together enables the teacher to share the construction of meaning with students so it becomes a "shared demonstration" (Routman, 2002). Copies of the text may be used by students during the lesson, but it is our belief that it is more effective to have all students focus on an enlarged text, even if they are going to continue to process the text later with a copy. Follow-up activities are not a necessary part of shared reading but can be used when they will help students extend their learning.

❖ **The text is read initially by the "expert," in most cases the teacher.**

He or she reads fluently and expressively and models phrasing, speed, and the use of punctuation. This also provides a scaffold for students who are below grade level in their reading. These students would struggle to process the text if they were reading it independently, but since they are freed from decoding and fluency, they are able to share in the construction of meaning from hearing and seeing the text at the same time. Readers who are at grade level or above may well be able to read with the teacher, and it is an instructional decision as to whether they are invited to join the reading on the first or the second read. When students do join in, the fluency should remain intact, and the reading becomes choral reading.

✤ **The selection of the text for shared reading is done by the teacher.**
While the text can be at different levels for different purposes, the most common way we select text is at grade level or slightly above grade level. This provides a manageable challenge for most students, and above-average readers will be reading the text, too. Above-grade-level students can still be challenged by the comprehension discussion that the teacher and students have about the text. Readers who are below grade level will see and process text that is grade and age appropriate. This is especially important as other parts of their reading instruction will be using instructional text at levels below grade level. While our remedial instruction works to bring our struggling students to grade level, it is important for these students to discuss and make meaning with grade-level texts.

Getting Started

> *How do I get started with interactive read-alouds? I'm overwhelmed!*

 Let's look at the decisions Val made before her lessons using *Amazing Bats* and *Killer Whales*.

Val knew that her students loved nonfiction. After several individual conferences, she realized they needed to understand that when they were reading nonfiction, they should not only think about what they knew about the topic but also be aware of when their thinking changed. Often, they held onto beliefs that weren't true and didn't know how to think through a text as they read so they could confirm what was actually true and change their thinking as they acquired new information. Val then looked for short, engaging nonfiction that could help her demonstrate how to confirm and change ideas about a topic during reading.

Her decisions about what to teach and the texts to use were based on her students' needs and interests, as well as her plan for reading for the year. She also considered which skills and strategies her second graders would need as they transitioned to longer texts and even to topics with which they were not familiar.

 ### Now, let's look at Rochelle's decisions regarding an interactive-read aloud in a fourth-grade classroom.

For an interactive read-aloud with fourth-grade students, Rochelle thinks carefully about a picture book that will be engaging and have content that can challenge these students to think in a deeper way about the story. She chooses *The Summer My Father Was Ten* (Brisson, 1999). This picture book is a flashback told by the father about his experience when he was ten and how his behavior embarrassed him. It tells of how the father gained forgiveness and how he learned to be a better person for the rest of his life. The short length is ideal for the first interactive read-aloud because students' level of engagement could be held. The book has captivating illustrations that use color to reinforce the emotions that the father feels.

Rochelle believes this would be a great book to use to model her thinking and encourage students to notice how she builds an understanding of the book's theme and main idea before, during, and after she reads it. She also decides to begin a chart about how important it is to think and be aware of our inner voice as we read. Rochelle wants all students to become aware of their inner voices, if they are not already, before she starts a strategy study.

These students have experienced many read-alouds, so they know the conventions of listening, partner discussion, and talking about the book. Rochelle needs to show them how interactive read-alouds would be a bit different.

Rochelle introduces *The Summer My Father Was Ten* to students, asking them to notice her thinking as she reads it aloud. She lets them know that today she will be thinking out loud as she reads. She assures students that in future interactive read-alouds she will invite them to share their thinking but that today their job is to learn how her thinking helps her as a reader. Rochelle then proceeds to read the text, stopping several times to think aloud for students. She knows that students need to hear the flow of the story as well as her thinking, though stopping more than several times during the reading would interrupt the flow of the story.

After the reading, Rochelle lists what students have noticed about her thinking as she read. This is a very informal assessment that allows a teacher to find out how much students understand and how often it will be necessary to model a particular strategy. Rochelle goes on to record her thinking before she read, during the reading, and after the reading. She discusses how her inner voice helps her think through a text so that she really gets a great understanding of the book. She explains this is important so that readers get to feel empathy for characters and become "lost in the story."

We have found it effective on the first day of introducing a strategy, structure, skill, or genre for the teacher to model his or her thinking for students. It is important to expose them to the language we are going to use to describe our thinking before we encourage them to begin practicing their own thinking. Once students can begin to articulate what they have seen us do, then we invite them to join us to interact with the text. (There are many things that go into the decisions about which strategies, genres, skills, and, structures to teach in grades 2–5, and we talk in more depth about these decisions in Chapters 2–5.)

Making Decisions About Texts and Time

Teachers are faced with many decisions throughout their busy days. They must look at their resources, schedules, and district mandates. In the previous two sections, we gave you a window into the decisions we made. Now, we will look at several things we consider when we choose a text and how much time to devote to each.

Choosing the Text

Are you engaged by the text on the right? Well, your students will be. Eeeooouu! They will be imagining themselves eating these delicacies—creating a mental image before you can say visualizing. Not all the texts we use are revolting, but in teaching older students, it does help to start with texts that are engaging. Engagement with the text is absolutely critical. Of course, we are ready to move to more serious texts as we build a sense of community.

"Edible Bugs—If you had been invited to a recent dinner party at the New York Entomological Society you would have feasted on the following: Sizzling crickets and veggie tempura. Warm wax worm fritters. Roasted Australian grubs. Mouthwatering mealworm pizza. And for dessert? Chocolate cricket pie. (Just can't get enough of that cricket pie!)"

— from *Oh Yuck: The Encyclopedia of Everything Nasty* (Masof, 2000)

As teachers, we make decisions all the time about whether to use a familiar (previously read) or unfamiliar text. We use an unfamiliar text when we're modeling certain comprehension strategies: monitoring for meaning, using schema, or questioning. When thinking about inferring, mental images, determining importance, or synthesizing, a familiar text or an unfamiliar one is equally effective. Modeling our thinking about a structure or a genre is easier if we use a familiar text. Our instruction can then dig deeper into that structure or genre.

Find texts that you love and that will allow you to model your thinking with your students. We look for texts that will stretch our students' thinking, not only about reading but also about the world around them. As we discussed earlier, the texts are often beyond what they might be able to read and understand independently. We also look for a variety of structures, genres, and authors. In subsequent chapters and in the Appendix, you will find some texts that we love and have found especially useful.

Time

We have found that 20 minutes is an ideal amount of time for an interactive read-aloud or shared reading to be effective. You won't do an interactive read-aloud or a shared reading every day, so it will probably take about two weeks for most of your students to move to practicing a strategy or skill in a small group and/or independently.

Building Vocabulary

By using interactive read-alouds and shared reading, we are able to create a common language and understanding with the whole class, which we can build upon as we move into small-group work or individual conferences. Ultimately, our goal is for students to independently use the strategies and skills that have been modeled. In shared reading, as we gradually release the responsibility for comprehending the text to students, we are able to assess which ones will need more support and which are able to begin practicing the strategy independently. Our small-group work and individual conferences enable us to support students and to gain access to their use of the strategy or skill.

The sample lessons on pages 26–28 include the first week of interactive and shared reading in Val's second-grade and third-grade classrooms, and in a fifth-grade classroom that Rochelle worked in. The goal of the first week in all these classrooms is for students to learn the routines and structures related to interactive and shared reading. In all the classrooms, we spend several days getting to know students as readers, helping them learn about the classroom library, and establishing routines for choosing "just right" books before the lessons included here began.

Parting Thoughts . . .

Student engagement is the key. As well as bringing in new texts with high-interest topics, we carefully select a text for the challenge inherent in it. A text that has the right amount of challenge will add to the engagement of the readers. In our interactive and shared reading, we will also be looking for texts that advance our students' learning. We want to work with texts that push their thinking to a level they are capable of reaching with assistance. Vygotsky (1978) refers to this as the zone of proximal development (ZPD). Our ultimate goal is to use interactive read-alouds and shared reading so that students can use the reading strategies and skills they learn when they independently read texts at their own level.

Val's Second-Grade Class

Day 1	Day 2	Day 3	Day 4	Day 5
Mini-lesson: Interactive read-aloud Text: _Chrysanthemum_ (Henkes, 1996)	**Mini-lesson: Discussion of how students will participate in an interactive read-aloud**	**Mini-lesson: Interactive read-aloud Text: _But Names Will Never Hurt Me_ (Waber, 1994)**	**Mini-lesson: Shared reading Text: "Giant Hearts," a poem from _Giant Children_ (Bagert, 2005)**	**Mini-lesson: Discussion of shared reading**
Val begins by saying, "We have been getting to know one another as readers, and now I would like you to think about this sentence: Readers think about what they are reading and have conversations about what they are thinking." Several students offer their ideas: "We talk about the books we are reading." "You need to think about how to say the words." "You shouldn't talk when you are reading." "I think about the cover so I know if I'll like the book." Then Val explains that readers think as they read. "Usually, you can't hear what people are thinking as they read, but today I am going to do my thinking out loud. I'm sure you'll be thinking about the story, too, as I read it, but today, instead of sharing your thinking, I want you to notice my thinking. I'll stop and wonder, notice the illustrations and how they interact with the text. I'll use language that shows how and why I fell in love with this book." After Val reads the book, having stopped four to five times to demonstrate her thinking, she will chart what her students have noticed about it.	Val talks about interactive read-alouds, such as the one yesterday, when students watched and listened to her thinking, and about shared reading, when they will interact with the text with her. Together, Val and students chart which behaviors are important when they are watching and listening to her: They talk about needing to listen to and follow the story and to listen to Val's thinking. Val then gets students to think about how they might interact with the text with her. They review what it means to turn and talk and how to jot down an idea. These will be two ways that students share their thinking with each other and with Val when they are interacting with a text together.	Val begins by reminding the class about yesterday's discussion of how they will participate in an interactive read-aloud. She says, "Today, I'll show you my thinking for the first part of this book. In the second half of the book, we'll use our turn-and-talk partners to share our thinking."	This is the first time that Val has used the overhead with the class, so some time is spent talking about using it. After going over the routines for when she uses the overhead or electronic camera, Val says, "Today, we are going to look at a text that I will read to you, and together we will think about its meaning. You will be able to see the text so you can follow along and read it to yourself." Val starts by first thinking about the title and then moving on to each stanza.	Val reminds the class that yesterday they used the overhead projector to read the poem "Giant Hearts." She asks students to turn and talk to their partners about what they did yesterday to understand the poem. After a few minutes, Val has the children share their ideas with the rest of the class. Together, they come up with the important ideas about shared reading and add them to the chart they started on Day 2. They now have created an anchor chart to guide their thinking about interactive read-alouds and shared reading.

Val's Third-Grade Class

Day 1	Day 2	Day 3	Day 4	Day 5
Mini-lesson: Interactive read-aloud Text: *More Than Anything Else* (Bradby, 1995)	**Mini-lesson:** Discussion of how students will participate in an interactive read-aloud	**Mini-lesson:** Interactive read-aloud Text: *Mr. George Baker* (Hest, 2007)	**Mini-lesson:** Shared reading Text: Blog entry from Pratie Place entitled "He waits on the porch for his teacher to pick him up (2005)."	**Mini-lesson:** Discussion of shared reading
Val begins by saying, "We have spent the last few days talking about our reading lives. We've shared where, when, and what we like to read. But I wonder if you have ever stopped to think about all that is going on in your head as you read? There are things we do that help us understand the text, and you might not even be aware of what you're doing. During this year, we are going to take notice of the thinking that will help us understand what we're reading, as well as get to understand ourselves as readers." She goes on to say, "Usually, you can't hear what someone is thinking as they read, but today I'm going to do my thinking out loud. I'm sure you'll be thinking about the story, too, as I read it, but today, instead of sharing your thinking, I want you to notice my thinking. I'll stop and wonder and notice the illustrations and how they interact with the text. I will use language that shows how I go about understanding and appreciating the text." After Val reads the book, stopping four to five times to demonstrate her thinking, she will chart what students have noticed.	Val talks about interactive read-alouds, such as the one yesterday, when students watched and listened to her thinking, and about shared reading, when they will interact with the text with her. Together, Val and her students chart which behaviors are important when they are watching and listening to her. They talk about needing to listen to and follow the story and to listen to Val's thinking. Val then gets students to think about how they might interact with the text with her. They review what it means to turn and talk and how to jot down an idea. These will be two ways that students share their thinking with each other and with Val when they are interacting with a text together.	Val begins by reminding the class about yesterday's discussion of how they will participate in an interactive read-aloud. She says, "Today, I'll show you my thinking for the first part of this book. In the second half of the book, we'll use our turn and talk partners to share our thinking."	This is the first time that Val has used the overhead with the class, so some time is spent talking about using it. After going over the routines for when she uses the overhead or electronic camera, Val says, "Today, we are going to learn how to look at a text that I will read to you, and together we will think about its meaning. You will be able to see the text so you can follow along and read it to yourself." Val starts by first thinking about the title and looking at the pictures in the article. It's not long before students begin to connect this article to yesterday's book, *Mr. George Baker.* At this level, Val wants to help students see how to use a strategy or skill across various types of texts.	Val asks students to come to the gathering area with a pencil, a clipboard, and two sticky notes. She reminds them that yesterday they used the electronic camera to read the blog entry, "He Waits on the Porch for His Teacher." She asks students to jot down on their sticky notes what they did yesterday to understand the article. After a few minutes, Val has them share their ideas. Together, they come up with the important ideas about shared reading and add this to the chart they started on Day 2. Val actually uses Jeff Wilhelm's language (see Figure 1.4, page 15) to help students understand their roles in both interactive read-alouds and shared reading. They now have created an anchor chart to guide their thinking.

Rochelle's Fifth-Grade Class

Day 1	Day 2	Day 3	Day 4	Day 5
Mini-lesson: Interactive read-aloud Text: *Thank You, Mr. Falker* (Polacco, 2001)	**Mini-lesson: Discussion Question: *What is your role during an interactive read-aloud, and how will this help you as a reader?***	**Mini-lesson: Interactive read-aloud Text: A piece about Jacqueline Woodson in *Speaking of Journals* (Graham, 1999)**	**Mini-lesson: Shared reading Text: An interview with Jacqueline Woodson from *Speaking of Journals* (Graham, 1999)**	**Mini-lesson: Discussion of shared reading**

Rochelle meets students in the comfortable space the teacher has created for them to gather and discuss books. She begins by saying, "The first few days of school, we have been talking about who we are as readers. We've discovered books we all like, times we really enjoy reading, and even the struggles we've had as readers. Through these discussions, we've charted all the things we actually do to understand what we are reading. This year, we're going to be thinking about how we can use these skills to take our understanding and discussions of text to a deeper level."

Rochelle then tells students that she will be reading a book by Patricia Polacco, an author who is already familiar to many of them. She goes on to say, "This book, *Thank You, Mr. Falker*, had a big impact on me the first time I read it. I would like to share with you the thinking I did before, during, and after reading it. I'd like you to notice the language I use and try to be aware of what you are thinking as I am reading." Rochelle proceeds to demonstrate her thinking, then invites students to talk about what she did and how it compared with their own thinking while she was reading the book.

Day 2

Rochelle writes the word *interactive* on the board and asks students what it means. After several students have shared their ideas, Rochelle says, "Yesterday, I was interacting with the text. What did you notice I was doing, and what were you doing?" Together, they chart what students noticed. They also talk about how it helped or hindered them as readers. They go on to talk about how students might interact with the text with Rochelle and ways they can share their thinking with one another. This discussion leads to the creation of an anchor chart that will guide students during interactive read-alouds.

Day 3

The teacher has been reading *Hush* (Woodson, 2006) during read-aloud. Rochelle gathers students to hear a piece written about Woodson. She tells them that often she thinks about a book differently after finding out more about the author. Then she invites students to share anything they know about Jacqueline Woodson. As it turns out, they know a bit, but they are eager to learn more. Rochelle then reads the article, thinking aloud about how Ms. Woodson's life has influenced her writing and connecting this article to the novel they're reading. Rochelle clearly demonstrates higher-level thinking about text-to-text connections and invites students to analyze this piece in relation to Ms. Woodson's novel.

Day 4

Rochelle has put the interview with Ms. Woodson on the electronic camera. Students are familiar with viewing texts with the camera, so they are not distracted by this technology. Rochelle says, "Today, we are going to look at this interview with Ms. Woodson. I am going to read it to you, but I invite you to read along with me. Our goal is to work together to see how we can connect the novel, *Hush*, the article about Ms. Woodson that we read yesterday, and this interview. We want to be aware of how these connections help us comprehend all three texts."

Day 5

Rochelle asks students to come to the gathering area and sit with their reading partner. They will need a clipboard, several sticky notes, and pencils. Rochelle asks students to think back to the interview with Jacqueline Woodson that they read yesterday. She tells the partners to jot down on their sticky notes what they did yesterday as they connected the interview to the Woodson novel they're reading and the article about her. Rochelle wants them to pay close attention to the process they went through as a group and in-dividually. After a few minutes, she asks several sets of partners to share what they have come up with. Together, Rochelle and her students create a chart indicating how working together to make meaning of a text can help them look at the text at more than one level. She actually uses Jeff Wilhelm's language (see Figure 1.4, page 15) to help students understand how interactive read-alouds and shared reading can help them use certain strategies and skills when they are reading independently.

Chapter 2

Building Deeper Comprehension With Interactive Read-Alouds and Shared Reading

Let's Join Rochelle in a Fourth-Grade Classroom

Rochelle has the opportunity to work with a fourth-grade class at an urban school. She visits them in September just as the school year is beginning. Rochelle decides to begin her reading with students by looking at the behaviors that help readers monitor for meaning, a comprehension strategy.

Rochelle chooses *Voices in the Park* (Browne, 1998) for an interactive read-aloud. This book is about a simple meeting in a park between a well-to-do woman, her son, and their dog, and an unemployed man, his daughter, and their dog. All the characters are portrayed as gorillas. The trip is told from the point of view of each participant, but what makes this book a challenge to comprehend is that Browne uses four different fonts, language modes, and perceptions of the park to express how each (non-canine) character feels about the world. On the first read, many older students are confused by this text. (Anthony Browne is an excellent author study for older grades: His books are complex, and he loves gorillas and symbolism!!) Rochelle begins: "Today we are going to start talking about how we monitor for meaning when we read. I'm going to write 'Monitoring for Meaning' at the top of our chart."

Rochelle asks students if they know what it means to monitor something. The students indicate that this is an unfamiliar term. Rochelle discusses its meaning, giving the example of a bus monitor or a lunch monitor. Soon, the students have a little understanding about monitoring. Rochelle hopes to build their understanding of the term over the series of lessons so she does not define it for them.

She continues, "Today I am going to talk about how I try to make sense or get meaning from this book, *Voices in the Park* by Anthony Browne. I find this book can be very confusing. I'm going to read it and talk out loud about my thinking. At the end of the book read-aloud, I want you to tell me the things I did to help myself understand the book as I read it."

Rochelle begins the read-aloud by looking at the cover and the blurb on the back of the book. "I am noticing there is a picture of a park and two gorillas on the front, and I think that the setting is the park, especially since the title is *Voices in the Park*."

A student interjects, "There are two dogs, too."

Rochelle nods. "Oh, and two dogs. Don't forget today that you are noticing how I am thinking about the book as I read. In future lessons, you'll share your thinking. The blurb on the back is very interesting and different. I can see four sentences in four different fonts."

Rochelle continues, "I'm a bit confused. This doesn't help me work out what's going to happen. I wonder if I will understand these sentences after I finish reading."

> **Why did Rochelle decide to begin with a lesson on monitoring for meaning?**

Monitoring for meaning is the comprehension strategy Rochelle usually uses to begin her reading instruction. Monitoring for meaning sets the expectation that we need to understand what we read in order to be really *reading*. The reading behaviors we articulate will be referred to often during the course of the year, especially when we read difficult text. The fourth-grade teacher and Rochelle have done some reading conferences on the self-selected books the students were reading to find out if and how they are monitoring for meaning. The students were able to talk about the basic plot but were missing the nuances of the text: the humor, the sadness, the characters' feelings and motivations, and the importance of the dialogue. They were, as many students at this grade level do, reading the words but weren't working at truly understanding the text. When they encountered words, phrases, and sentences that they didn't understand, they just kept reading on.

We will come back later in the chapter to these fourth-grade students. Now, since there are many comprehension strategies to teach in addition to monitoring for meaning, we'll talk about how to teach systematically and strategically to cover all the reading strategies we need to teach.

Developing a Plan for Teaching Comprehension Strategies

> **Should every grade level work in depth with each comprehension strategy?**

We have grappled with this question with many groups of teachers and have come to see that it is more effective to concentrate on teaching three or four comprehension strategies each year while practicing strategies from previous years.

We created the Comprehension Strategies Big Hits chart below, and many school districts have found it useful. It's important for each district to think about how it will plan this instruction. Although we have listed the strategies in a particular order, we believe that after monitoring for meaning, the order of the other strategies is flexible.

Figure 2.1

COMPREHENSION STRATEGIES BIG HITS

Grade Level	Strategy
1st	Monitoring for Meaning Schema Asking Questions Creating Mental Images
2nd	Monitoring for Meaning Inferring Determining Importance Schema
3rd	Monitoring for Meaning Asking Questions Synthesizing Creating Mental Images
4th	Monitoring for Meaning Determining Importance Schema Inferring
5th	Monitoring for Meaning Inferring Asking Questions Synthesizing

> *These are thoughtful terms, but what do they mean when it comes to actually working with students?*

As we said earlier, **monitoring for meaning** is important at every level. First and foremost, students have to be able to recognize when what they are reading doesn't make sense. As we work with students, we need to help them identify when meaning breaks down. This might be due to their lack of understanding of a word, a phrase, or a whole section of a text. We need to model rereading and have students practice it, thinking about the context of the word or phrase, asking questions, and adjusting the rate of their reading as it relates to the difficulty and purpose of the reading.

Determining importance is bigger, in our minds, than identifying the main idea. Our schema, opinions, and experiences influence what we see as important in a text. As teachers, we model what we see as important in a text and why we feel this way. Students must be able to support their own thinking about what is important with examples from the text. Modeling our thinking about the author's purpose will also help students as they work to determine the important ideas in a text.

Our students also need to see how and why certain words or phrases may be more important than others in helping us understand the text. Bold print, italics, and even the size of the font can direct us to important words. And often, the first and last sentence in a nonfiction passage clue us in to important ideas.

Modeling all these reading behaviors together as we decide what is important in the text helps our students visualize using these behaviors in their own reading. Readers use all of their senses while **creating mental images**. We need to show students how the images we create help us understand the text. We also have to help students see that each of us will use our own experiences and the details in the text to create our own unique images.

Synthesizing is much easier to understand when you think of it as the way your thinking grows as you add and put together new ideas about a topic. It is not retelling the story or giving a summary. Synthesizing involves more abstract thinking. We often model for students how we reflect, draw conclusions, and develop a personal understanding of the journey our thinking takes as we discover new things about a character, setting, structure, or topic. The end result of the journey is the ability to put all the elements together to synthesize our thinking.

Schema is simply our background knowledge. When talking to our students, we like to refer to schema as the filing cabinet in our brain. We talk about the folders we create to store our experiences and previously learned information. Activating our schema before

BUILDING INDEPENDENT READERS © 2011 by Valorie Falco and Rochelle P. Soloway • Scholastic Teaching Resources

we read is especially important when we are reading nonfiction. We help students understand the way our schema changes and grows as we continue to learn. Val has two lessons in Chapter 1 that demonstrate this strategy (see pages 16–18).

Questioning is what proficient readers do, almost automatically, but many students don't have this running monologue of questions going through their heads as they read. We want to help students focus their reading by asking questions before, during, and after they read. We're not talking about a series of literal comprehension questions that often don't even require the student to read the text. We're talking about the authentic questions a reader asks herself as she reads—questions such as "Why did the character do that?" or "What is the character thinking?" or "Now, what will they do?" These are the questions that lead to a deeper understanding of the text.

Inferring includes a variety of skills. Students are inferring when they are making predictions or drawing conclusions. This strategy requires students to blend what is stated in the text with their own ideas and background knowledge. We often tell students: "You need to use what's on the page and what's in your head together to infer."

How do you work through a series of lessons on a comprehension strategy?

 Let's return to Rochelle and the fourth-grade class.

After Rochelle reads the first page of *Voices in the Park*, she says, "I think I will read that again. I'm not exactly sure of what is happening. I also want to work out which character is Victoria and which is Charles. It seems odd to me that the mother is speaking nicely to the dog and not to her son."

Rochelle rereads the page and clarifies that the dog is Victoria, and indeed, the mother is speaking pleasantly to the dog and commandingly to Charles, her son. Rochelle comments, "I really need to work out the names of the characters when I read. I understand the story much better then."

As Rochelle reads, she uses expression to match the emotive and unique language each character uses. She talks to the students as she does: "I am noticing that the mother is speaking very rudely about the dog that is playing with her dog, Victoria. She calls it a 'scruffy mongrel.' She also speaks rudely about the little girl gorilla who sits near her son, Charles. I think it's very important to read the text the way the character would say this. It helps me understand the book if I use expression."

As Rochelle reads each section of the book, labeled "First Voice," "Second Voice," "Third Voice," and "Fourth Voice," she uses different voices to emphasize the varied language modes of each character. She continues to discuss this as she reads on.

Rochelle also thinks out loud about the way the park is illustrated differently in each section and how strange the shapes are for the trees and streetlights: "I am noticing that although the park is in each section, it looks totally different. The colors are changing. Let's look through the book and look at the changes. I am noticing that when the unemployed father is talking, the park looks black and brown and dead. I can see his newspaper very clearly, though. I wonder why the author/illustrator did this? It seems to me that the colors might be showing us how the characters are feeling."

The students listen quietly and seem enthralled by this complex picture book. After Rochelle finishes reading and talking about her thinking, she invites students to tell her what they noticed her doing to understand what she was reading. She lists these behaviors on the chart (see Figure 2.2).

After Rochelle writes the reading behaviors down, she congratulates the students on their observations. She knows from the discussion that the class needs to continue to work on this strategy before they gain full understanding of how to apply it.

At the end of the lesson, Rochelle asks students if they think they know what happened in the book. Most are still con-

Figure 2.2

Monitoring for Meaning

- Go back and look at pictures
- Ask questions
- Read carefully
- Reread: check names, try to follow

fused, but one student says, "I think maybe they are visiting the park in different seasons." Rochelle and the students look at the pictures to confirm this and discover that this could be a viable explanation. Rochelle knew at the onset that this was a confusing book, but she is a bit surprised that after modeling her thinking her students don't realize the four voices are talking about their own versions of the same event, and they are not confident in their understanding of the book. Rochelle refers students back to the chart. She explains that when we are not sure about what is happening in a book, a good behavior is to read it again. "Tomorrow, I am going to read this book again to build on our thinking. Some books are hard to understand, and we need to read them more than once."

The students agree and are eager to hear the book again. For these students, the notion of rereading is quite a powerful one.

> ### It doesn't sound like the lesson went as Rochelle planned. Now what will she do?

There was a change in what Rochelle expected to do. She had thought the students would understand this book in one session and had planned to do an interactive read-aloud with a new picture book the next day. When you invite students to tell you what they notice or are thinking, they don't always come up with what you are expecting, but their response is what should drive instruction. Rochelle knew this book had fascination for the students and she could use it to further their understanding about how readers monitor for meaning.

 ## Rochelle's second lesson using monitoring for meaning with *Voices in the Park*

At the beginning of the second session, Rochelle discusses what monitoring for meaning can mean when someone is reading. One student describes it as patrolling for meaning. Rochelle adds this to the chart.

During the second reading of the book, Rochelle continues to talk about her thinking. She also allows students to speak about what they are thinking during the reading. The symbolism in the illustrations strongly grabs their attention. Rochelle directs them back to the change in font and color: "I am thinking that the fonts are very important. I think the color change, which is dramatic, is important, too. I wonder why the author/illustrator did this?"

The students continue to notice the colors and even direct Rochelle back to a page where the two children gorillas are sitting together: In this illustration, it is sunny at one end of the park bench and cloudy and grey at the other. Students begin to articulate the connection between color and emotion.

Rochelle then poses the question "Well, what happened in the story?" She is confident someone will discuss that the event is the same for all the voices but that the characters see it differently because of how they view the world (Rochelle's interpretation!). Students indicate they are still puzzled and don't know exactly how the book works. Rochelle deliberately doesn't tell them, but knows that later in the year they will return to the book to look at it again.

Rochelle's plan for the series of lessons changed significantly as she interacted with the students. She decides instead of moving to shared reading, she needs to continue with interactive read-alouds because the students need stronger scaffolding. Which follow-up book will have the most impact? Rochelle decides upon *Dear Mrs. LaRue: Letters from Obedience School* (Teague, 2002). She thinks the change to a humorous book will engage students as they discuss the use of color to portray the dog's perception of his stay in the Obedience School and the real situation.

Unfortunately, during the lesson, Rochelle finds that the persuasive language used by the dog is not language these students understand easily. The dog's conversation revolves around words such as *misconceptions, melodramatic, lummox,* and *queasy.*

Rochelle adds the following behavior to the monitoring for meaning chart: "Sometimes we need to understand a particular word to understand what we are reading." While that behavior is important, Rochelle had hoped to go further with Teague's book and monitoring for meaning behaviors. However, the students didn't engage with the book and were too confused to work on this deeper comprehension. The lesson's being held on a Friday afternoon at the end of the first week of school may well have contributed to this. Not all lessons will go as smoothly as you would like!

 ## Rochelle goes back to the drawing board to conduct her fourth interactive read-aloud.

Over the weekend, Rochelle rethinks her lesson plans and decides that *The Emperor's Egg,* a Read and Wonder book (Jenkins, 2002), would be an engaging interactive read-aloud with the fourth-grade students. This is a nonfiction book about emperor penguins; it has a running narrative text, and wavy lines of facts about penguins are written in a different font and supported by beautiful, colorful drawings.

Rochelle introduces turn-and-talk to students, and partners move near each other so they can share their thinking about the book when she asks them to. She knows that with this book she cannot get students to simply listen to her thinking. They will be eager to begin to share and interact.

The students are immediately fascinated by these amazing creatures. They marvel that penguins waddle 100 miles to arrive at their breeding grounds. They are impressed by the father penguin's looking after the egg for two months with nothing to eat. The language in the book and the way it is set out as a nonfiction literary piece captivates students. Rochelle continues to model the reading behaviors that help her understand what she is reading. She discusses how to read the narrative and facts so the facts don't interrupt the flow of the narrative. She models how to read text that is larger than the rest of the text. She marvels over these fascinating animals and how she is adding to what she knows about them. The lesson goes very well, and from students' comments and questions, Rochelle now knows that students are finally beginning to understand the reading behaviors they need to use when they are reading texts of their own choosing.

Figure 2.3

Monitoring for Meaning
"Patrolling"

- Go back and look at pictures
- Ask questions
- Read carefully
- Reread: check names, try to follow
- Sometimes we need to understand a particular word
- Decide how to read different parts so it still makes sense
- Take notice of the writing (fonts)
- Think about what you know
- Talk about new information

Additions Rochelle made to the "Monitoring for Meaning" chart after reading aloud Dear Mrs. LaRue *and* The Emperor's Egg

Of course, there is more work to do, but Rochelle knows students are now using the vocabulary of monitoring for meaning and beginning to expect meaning every time they read. This gives her the opportunity to select texts for shared reading.

Releasing Responsibility to Students:
Shared Reading on Monitoring for Meaning

Considering the students and their needs in reading instruction, Rochelle is looking for texts that are short and very engaging to use for their shared reading lessons. Thinking about the deeper structures described by Ellin Keene (see page 10), Rochelle knows it is important to work on developing students' pragmatic systems. They are not in the habit of being readers. They see reading as a chore, something to endure rather than to enjoy. It is important to captivate these readers in pieces of text that challenge them to think but at the same time interest them. Rochelle will move to more complex texts as the year progresses.

The first text Rochelle uses to practice monitoring for meaning behaviors is "Ezekiel Johnson" by Walter Dean Myers. This short story about a homeless man appears in *Thanks and Giving All Year Long* (Thomas & Cerf, 2004). It takes twists and turns, and it tests our ideas about being homeless. Rochelle explains that Myers challenges us to consider what it means to be "more than what you own."

Another good text for a first shared reading lesson on monitoring for meaning would be a short piece from *Oh, Yuck! The Encyclopedia of Everything Nasty* (Masoff, 2000). The introductory paragraph to each new topic is written descriptively and uses vocabulary that would challenge most students in the intermediate grades. The selection "Edible Bugs" is just one of the examples that will grab students' attention (see page 23). There are many topics to choose from in the book that will have your students highly engaged (mostly because they are so gross) and collaboratively working with you to understand what they are reading.

We recommend using very short pieces to model the behaviors students are learning to control. In this teaching environment, the focus is not on learning about leeches, naked mole-rats, or the strange foods other people eat; it's about practicing monitoring behaviors so they become automatic. These lessons are short, sharp, and focused on monitoring for meaning.

Another interesting piece to use for monitoring for meaning is "King Tut: Modern Science Comes Face-to-Face With an Ancient Mystery" (*National Geographic Explorer*, September 2005). Many of these types of articles can be accessed at the *National Geographic Explorer* archives at http://magma.nationalgeographic.com/ngexplorer/archive.

Rochelle chose the article on King Tut because it has multiple text features for students to navigate with her: photographs, maps, short facts, running text—and it involves a mummy and a murder mystery! There are many resources available in your school library or on the Internet that will provide this type of text. With electronic cameras and interactive whiteboards in many classrooms, the access and enlargement of these articles is considerably easier for teachers.

Rochelle continues to model and think aloud at times during shared reading, but turn and talk, recording thinking on sticky notes, charting thinking, and using graphic organizers become an integral part of the lessons.

What does releasing responsibility for monitoring for meaning look like?

 Let's join Rochelle and the fourth-grade students in a shared reading lesson of a short story.

Rochelle introduces the short story "Ezekiel Johnson" to students by displaying a full-page illustration on the electronic camera: "Today, we are going to read a short story by Walter Dean Myers about a homeless man named Ezekiel Johnson. As you look at this picture of Ezekiel standing in a shopping cart, what are you thinking? Does this picture help you get an idea about the story? I would like you to turn and talk to your partner about what you're thinking."

After several minutes, Rochelle asks several partners to share their thinking about the picture.

"I remember seeing homeless people pushing shopping carts with all their stuff in it. It's weird that he's in the cart, not his stuff."

"We can't figure out why he's standing with his hands that way, and the cart looks bigger than he does."

The responses show that some students have images of shopping carts and homeless people, while others make observations about the cart and Ezekiel with no connection to being homeless.

Rochelle responds, "The picture got some of you thinking about the homeless people you've seen, but it doesn't really give us an idea of what the story will be about. Your observation about the cart being bigger than Ezekiel makes me think that the cart will play a big part in this story."

Then Rochelle uses the electronic camera to share the first paragraph of the story. She encourages the students to read, aloud or silently, with her. From this paragraph, students learn that Ezekiel lives in a big city and uses the shopping cart to collect cans. They also find out that he lives in a cardboard house in an alley behind a theater—an alley that he keeps clean.

"This first paragraph seems like a brief introduction to Ezekiel," Rochelle comments. "Since the theater is mentioned, I think it will be important to the story."

Rochelle puts up the next paragraph and reads it to students. Then she says, "Wow, how many of you expected the alley to belong to Ezekiel?"

Students are surprised that a homeless man owns land. They can't understand why Ezekiel is homeless if he owns the land.

Rochelle continues, "Now that we know Ezekiel has been paid for the land and has fourteen thousand dollars, it seems that his life is going to change. Turn and talk to your partner about what you think will happen."

Most students believe Ezekiel will get a place to live. Some think he will buy a house, but others think he will rent an apartment. Everyone is sure Ezekiel will get all kinds of things he doesn't have, such as a TV and a bed.

Rochelle reveals and reads aloud the next three paragraphs. None of the students expected Ezekiel to give the money away.

"Why did he do that?"

"He's crazy."

"What does he mean, 'A man ain't just what he owns'? He doesn't own anything."

Rochelle listens to their comments and then says, "Okay, the story has really changed, and now we have a lot of different thoughts about Ezekiel."

Students agree that the last three paragraphs did change their thinking and that it would have been important to stop and listen to what their inner voice was telling them if they were reading the story independently.

Rochelle emphasizes this point: "When we are reading, we need to stop and take notice of places like this in stories. They are really important. When the story is going the way we expect, we can just read through these parts. So, today we learned we have to stop for a moment and think about a big change or new information that is brought into the writing."

Rochelle and the students read the rest of the story. They relate to the reporter who is interviewing Ezekiel and trying to understand why he bought coats for everyone and nothing for himself. The line about being more than you own comes up again.

   BUILDING INDEPENDENT READERS © 2011 by Valorie Falco and Rochelle P. Soloway • Scholastic Teaching Resources

She asks the students to turn and talk: "Talk about why you think Ezekiel did what he did and what he means when he says, 'Means you got to be more than what you own.'"

After the discussion, which shows that students are beginning to see why Ezekiel did what he did, Rochelle asks them to use a sticky note during their independent reading to mark any part where they need to stop and think carefully about what they are reading— a big change or new information.

Using the Comprehension Strategies Big Hits to Plan Units

When we began using interactive and shared reading to model how the comprehension strategies help us better understand a text, our lessons were all over the place— monitoring for meaning one week, questioning another week, and something totally different the next week. The lessons were good, but because we jumped around, our students often struggled with using the strategies independently. We began planning out units of study, sticking with one strategy over time, and gradually releasing more and more responsibility to students— and we began to see our students use these strategies more independently.

Over time, as we worked with more and more teachers, it became apparent that we needed to take our thinking about the comprehension strategies a step further. When we tried to do all the strategy units in a year, certain units got shortchanged, we didn't spend as much time as our students needed on a strategy, or we simply didn't get to certain strategies because we ran out of time. That led us to think about concentrating on only three or four strategies each year. By setting up a schoolwide plan to explicitly teach certain strategies at each grade level, we found that all the strategies were being taught and a common language was being used, not just in one classroom but across grade levels.

Do you always begin with the monitoring for meaning strategy?

As we said before, we think monitoring for meaning is a good strategy to start off the school year. Each year, students will be faced with new text types, text structures, and texts of increasing length and difficulty. Classrooms will have new students who may not be familiar with the language and behaviors associated with monitoring their own understanding of the text. Starting the year with a unit on monitoring for meaning helps establish your classroom as a community of learners who know that reading is not "barking at the print" (saying the words without an understanding of what is being read) but is about thinking and making meaning from the text.

This is true for Val even though she is looping her second graders to third grade, and they looked at this strategy at the beginning of second grade. She knows these readers, and it is time to apply this strategy to higher-level texts and even texts that may not be quite so engaging. It is also time for these readers to begin to think more about what they will do to recognize when meaning breaks down. Both of these skills will be important as readers at this level begin to read more texts in which they will be asked to understand information for which they have no schema.

The chart on page 27 lays out Val's first week of interactive read-alouds and shared reading mini-lessons for third grade. It explains how Val gets her students thinking about the role of interactive and shared reading in their classroom and indicates that she has chosen *More Than Anything Else* (Bradby, 1995) as her first interactive read-aloud of the year. She is using this text because she knows her students have little if any schema for understanding the time period, the 1860s, and certainly no schema for understanding the young boy's life, one in which he spends each day shoveling salt. She also wants to begin exploring the idea of wanting, more than anything else, the opportunity to learn— something her students take for granted. Val is layering her lessons on interactive read-alouds and shared reading with lessons on monitoring for meaning. She's able to do this multitasking because she already knows her students. If this were a new group of third graders, Val would have separated the concepts, using one group of texts to model the interactive read-aloud and another set to model the strategy of monitoring for meaning.

The mini-lesson charts in Chapter 1 show a five-day sequence, but Val continues exploring monitoring for meaning for the next two weeks. She uses a variety of texts to model for her students how to negotiate texts for which they have little or no schema. She also demonstrates what she does to read and understand difficult texts. Together, she and her students work to create two anchor charts, one showing the skills to use to read through difficult texts (see Figure 2.4 on page 43) and one showing how to determine when meaning breaks down and what to do to fix it (see Figure 2.5 on page 43). The goal is for students to monitor for meaning when they are reading independently. Displaying both of these charts will provide them with visual reminders throughout the year.

Figure 2.4

What Do Readers Do When Reading Through a Difficult Text?

- Reread
- Slow down
- Ask questions:

    What does that mean?

    Why did that happen?

    What does the author want me to know or understand?

- Talk to self about what is going on
- Make brief notes

Figure 2.5

How Do You Know When You're Not Understanding What You're Reading— Meaning Has Broken Down?

→ How Do You Fix It?

- I lost my place. → Go back and reread.
- I get to the end of the page, and I don't know what I read. → Go back to the top of the page and reread.
- I don't know who is talking. → Think about the characters and what is happening—who could be saying it—then reread with that character in mind.

How long do you usually stay on a strategy?

This is a hard question because so much depends on your students. If you have students who have been in classrooms that worked on strategy instruction, they will probably have the language needed to talk about their thinking. You might need to spend only two days on interactive read-alouds, but delve into more complex short texts in shared reading. The move from interactive to shared reading will be based on your observations of your students. It is important to give students the time they need to internalize the language and to engage in conversations that will move their thinking to a deeper level. Once you begin to see them using the strategy with you during shared reading, it is time to have them practice the strategy independently. Overall, for your average learner, it will take about three weeks to move from watching you model the strategy to using it independently with a variety of texts.

 ### The next strategy unit for Val's third graders is mental images.

During writing conferences with her third-grade students, Val notices she is repeatedly talking to them about adding details that help readers create pictures in their head as they are reading. Although Val knows her students can talk about creating mental images when they read, she begins to wonder if they have really understood how this strategy can help them as readers, and the implication of this strategy for them as writers.

The next day at the beginning of reading, the students gather on the rug. Each child has a clipboard and sticky notes. Val has a copy of *Andrew Lost on the Dog* (Greenberg, 2002), which was a read-aloud at the beginning of the year. She puts the book on the electronic camera, turns to the chapter where follicle mites are described in great detail, and then says, "Do you remember when we read this book back in September? When we got to this part, many of us actually started to rub our eyes. Why did we do that?"

Students start to talk about how, while reading this particular passage, they actually thought they could feel the mites on their eyelashes even though they knew they couldn't.

Val continues, "Today, we are going to do a shared reading of the text, thinking about the way J. C. Greenberg wrote this section, so we can 'feel' those miniscule mites. I know a lot of us got some pretty gross pictures in our minds the first time we read it, but how do those pictures actually help us understand the text? Why is it so important to 'see' and 'feel' this part of the text?"

After reading this section of the book, Val leaves the text up and has students jot down words that help them see what is in the text. Several students share their words and phrases and then Val asks, "But why does seeing these images help us understand this text?"

She has partners turn and talk about what they are thinking. As Val listens, she hears them talking about being in the book—the author "transported me to those follicles"—and the idea that they actually could imagine being the main characters Andrew and Judy. In the discussion that then takes place with the whole group, Val helps students chart what the author did and why it helped them as readers. One of the students sums it up by saying, "When I am standing there right next to the character, it's not just the picture that helps me, but the way the picture makes me feel. I am sucked into being on the adventure with the character, wondering what will happen next."

Later, Val will use this chart for her mini-lesson in writing so that students see clearly the reading-writing connection.

 ## Three months into the year, Val tackles synthesizing with her third graders.

Val, like many teachers, has shied away from synthesizing with either her second or third graders because it involves more abstract thinking and is not as easy to model or explain as the other comprehension strategies. She decides it's time to introduce this higher-level strategy to her third graders. Since she always begins the school year familiarizing her students with reading a series together in the classroom, Val thinks she can go a step further and help her students understand synthesizing as a way to comprehend a text. Her goal will be for students to think about how the characters' motives and actions in one book in the series can help them think about what the character might do in subsequent books. As students read more books in the series, their ideas about the characters' actions and reactions will grow and change.

Val and the class gather on the rug. All around them are baskets. Each basket contains the books in a particular series that students have read in second or third grade. Val starts, "Last year, and so far this year, we have spent a lot of time reading books in a series." She puts up the anchor chart they started in second grade that lists their thinking about how reading a series helps them as readers (see Figure 2.6 on page 46).

Figure 2.6

How Does Reading a Series Help You as a Reader?

- After I read the first book, I can think about what will be happening in the next book.
- I can think about how the stories are connected—if I can't understand the connection because I'm reading random books in the series, I know I have to read the books in order.
- The longer the series, the more I'm able to think about what will happen next.
- When I've read one series and then I start another series, I think about how they're the same or I connect them to another series I've read.
- As I read more and more books in a series, I get better at figuring out the words.
- When I read a series, I try to think about how what's happening in this series is different from other series I've read.
- When I read random books not in a series, my thinking gets all mixed up. When I read in a series, I'm not as confused.
- When I started reading, I was shy about picking books. I didn't know the words or what was happening, but I got hooked on a series, and I felt like I could know the words and what was going on.
- Because I kept reading *Babymouse*, I started to figure out where things started and stopped. The first one was hard, but after reading a lot of them, it's a snap.
- When I started, I read really, really fast, but I figured out I missed a lot of details. Now I read slower so I catch all the details throughout the scenes.
- By rereading a series, I started to really understand what was going on.
- Reading more books in a series makes it more interesting.

 BUILDING INDEPENDENT READERS© 2011 by Valorie Falco and Rochelle P. Soloway • Scholastic Teaching Resources

Val goes on to say, "This chart helped us last year as we were thinking about reading a series. I am wondering if our thinking about series will grow and change this year. Today, I am going to read to you the beginning of a new book in a series you are familiar with, *Roscoe Riley Rules #6: Never Walk in Shoes That Talk* (Applegate, 2009). Before I start, I am going to think about what I know about Roscoe and the structure the author uses in this series. I know each book starts with Roscoe in Time Out. In fact, the author titles this part 'Welcome From Time Out' in each book. The other chapters that are always in this series are 'Something You Should Know Before We Get Started,' 'Something Else You Should Know Before We Get Started,' and 'Good-bye From Time Out.' I will be expecting these to be part of this book, too. I also know Roscoe starts out with a good idea and is surprised when it doesn't work out quite the way he thinks it will. He always ends up getting into trouble. I will be expecting this to be true in this book, too."

Val reads the beginning of the book, confirming that what she thought about the structure of the book and Roscoe is true. She stops after four pages and says, "So although I haven't read this whole book yet, I can see that Roscoe starts out trying to help his friend. However, like in other books, he doesn't really think through the consequences. I am wondering if there will ever be a time in one of these books when Roscoe thinks about what has happened in the past. I think having Roscoe think about a plan and its consequences might change the way the series works and maybe I would lose interest. I actually want Roscoe to learn from his mistakes, but I am never disappointed when he doesn't. Thinking about what I know of Roscoe and my own experiences with learning from my mistakes helps me imagine how the stories might change. I am able to recommend these books, not just by re-telling the story to you but also by synthesizing, putting what I know from my life and what I know about Roscoe together like a puzzle."

Thus, Val has done an introduction to synthesizing. Tomorrow, she will actually do a shared reading of a book review of one of the books in a series students love in order to help them see that by synthesizing we actually come to understand the text better.

 ## Next, Val will begin a unit on the questioning strategy.

Later in the year, Val's third graders are working on having conversations about the books they read as part of a small group. Val wants them thinking about the questions that keep the conversation going and those that don't. Her decision about working on the questioning strategy is based not just on a pacing calendar but also on the needs of her students. Val is going to use her interactive read-alouds and shared reading to model the questioning she does as she reads. She hopes these will be a springboard for the questioning the students do on their own and when they come together to discuss a book. Val does her first interactive read-aloud with a wonderful book about Thanksgiving, *Rivka's First Thanksgiving* (Rael, 2001).

Several days later, Val is ready to invite students to interact with the text with her. For this interactive read-aloud, she chooses *You and Me and Home Sweet Home* (Lyon, 2009), which is about homelessness. Val is sure there will be a lot of thought-provoking questions due to the nature of the story. The class comes to the rug with clipboards, sticky notes, and pencils. Val begins by showing the class the front and back covers and reading the back cover of the book. She chooses not to read the blurb on the flap so the story and students' questions will unfold as she reads. As they look at the end pages, Val comments, "Wow, the front end pages are very different from the back end pages. I am sure the authors did this on purpose, but I wonder how many people actually look at the front and back before they start to read the book. I know that often I don't, and yet reading these pages made me think about what was going to happen in the story. Looking at these pages, I ask myself what brought about such a big change in the girl's expression. This question actually gets my brain geared up to read the book."

After reading the first page, Val says, "This page gives us a lot of information, both in the text and the illustration. I have so many questions. I wonder where Uncle Al is. They have been living in the back room for over a year, but now they are between a rock and a hard place."

Before Val can go on, one of the students says, "But what does 'between a rock and a hard place' mean?" They talk about this expression, and Val can see students begin to understand why the little girl and her mother are in a difficult place. Although students have no idea why the girl and her mother have lived with Aunt Janey for over a year or where Uncle Al has been, they do understand that the little girl and her mother have no place to live. At this point, Val asks students to write down a question they are really wondering about. After several minutes, she asks several students to share their questions.

"Why are their clothes in sacks?"

"Does she have any toys?"

"What's the girl's name?"

"Where are they going to live when Uncle Al comes home?"

"What are they going to do now?"

"Where's her mom work?"

Val writes these questions on a chart. She is pleased some students are asking questions that cannot be easily answered and that will drive them to think about the text as she reads on. Since Val wants to help her students move beyond very literal questions, she takes the opportunity to say, "As you can see, there are a lot of different questions we can be asking before we continue to read. Some seem to make a difference in how the story progresses, and some seem to stay the same regardless of what happens in the story. Let's look at your questions. Which ones do you think will make a difference in how the story progresses, and which ones will stay the same regardless of what happens in the story?"

Together, they look at the questions and decide the ones that will matter most are "Where are they going to live when Uncle Al comes home?" and "What are they going to do now?"

Val says, "I think you've noticed an important thing about the questions we ask ourselves as we read and discuss books: Some questions help us better understand the story because they push us to think more about the story. Others are very specific. They help us notice specific details, but they are not really up for discussion."

Val continues reading the book to the class. She periodically stops and has students write down a question they are wondering about. As they read and discover some of the answers to their questions, they begin to see how some questions just seem bigger and more important to understanding the book. Over the next few days, Val and the class will look at questioning through shared reading and their book discussion groups.

Is that all the comprehension strategy work for the year?

 ### No, now it is time to integrate our strategy instruction.

We focus our instruction on one strategy at a time so students have time to apply and extend the strategy to their own reading. But as Regie Routman points out in *Reading Essentials* (2002), "When we read, we simultaneously and seamlessly employ a whole range of strategies, and we are constantly making refinements and adjustments according to the demands of the text and what we bring to it. Our comprehension process is invisible and difficult to document. So while it is useful to practice a strategy as students are learning it, make sure that most of your comprehension instruction uses strategies interactively" (p. 129). Helping our students use multiple strategies will be the focus for the rest of the year. We will use interactive read-alouds and shared reading to model the invisible process of comprehending a text using multiple strategies.

Let's return to Val's third-grade classroom.

The year is half over, and Val knows her students can talk the talk regarding comprehension strategies, and in isolation things go quite well. But . . . now it is time for her students to become aware of how those strategies work together to deepen their understanding of the text. Val has brought a toolbox to school. It is filled with various tools: several hammers, wrenches, screwdrivers, a drill, a tape measure, and a small saw. She holds it up and asks students what it is. Several know it is a toolbox. As they look together at the tools, many students are at least somewhat familiar with the tools and what each does. Now Val asks, "Which one is most important if you are going to build or fix something?"

"The saw."

"No, the hammer."

"Maybe the screwdriver."

Finally one student asks, "What are you fixing?"

Val asks, "Does it matter?"

The discussion continues, and soon students come to an agreement: The tool you need most depends on what you are building or fixing, and most of the time, you will need to use several tools together.

This is the perfect lead-in for Val to talk about using a "toolbox" for comprehending a text. She reviews with students all the anchor charts they have created so far this year. She then brings out a paper toolbox she has created. She tells students that this is their comprehension toolbox. She points out that just like the tools needed to fix a bike are different than the tools needed to build a house, so the tools needed to comprehend a text will

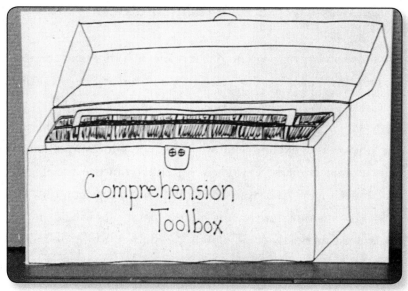

Val's Comprehension Toolbox

not always be the same. Also, just as more than one tool is needed to build a house, more that one strategy is needed to fully understand a text. This is the mini-lesson that begins Val's work on using multiple comprehension strategies.

 Val begins an interactive read-aloud on integrating comprehension strategies.

Val is excited to share a new book, *The Last Polar Bear* (George, 2009), with her students. This book is wonderful for demonstrating the natural thinking one does about a text, thinking that is not focused on one strategy but that interweaves a variety of strategies to better understand and appreciate a text. Val's interactive read-aloud models her thinking about what she knows about the author and, therefore, what she will be expecting in the book, the questions that arise as she reads, and the images that are created by parts of the text. As she models, she is making all her thinking visible to her students.

Val will continue throughout the year using interactive read-alouds and shared reading to help her students clearly see that reading is thinking, across all strategies.

Parting Thoughts . . .

If you are thinking that teaching the deeper comprehension strategies is hard work, you are right. These interactive read-alouds and shared reading lessons require thoughtful planning and careful use of questioning and prompting techniques by the teacher. Not all lessons are successful, and as we have demonstrated, sometimes lessons need to be repeated frequently before the teacher can begin to notice that students are able to use the vocabulary and actions needed to build the thought processes. This persistence by the teacher, the school, and the district will reap the benefits of having readers that independently use the three deeper structure systems that we discussed in Chapter 1 (see pages 10–12).

Moving from interactive read-aloud (I do, you watch) to shared reading (I do, you help) is a decision the teacher makes based upon feedback from students during lessons. When the teacher first begins interactive read-alouds focused on a new strategy, he or she begins with thinking aloud to establish the vocabulary and reading behaviors. After several sessions of thinking aloud, then the teacher invites students to interact with the text. Once the teacher observes students using the reading behaviors and vocabulary in this setting, it is time to begin releasing some of the responsibility to them via shared reading. Shared reading allows the teacher to see when students are able to practice the behaviors and vocabulary with less support. Collaborative thinking during shared reading is a powerful way to move students to independence.

Assessment of what students have learned is accomplished by listening and interacting with them during whole-group, small-group, and individual interactions. The feedback you receive from your students will drive the next piece of your instruction. Many reading behaviors take a period of time for students to understand and use effectively.

Lessons need to build upon one another, and it is the sequence of interactions with texts, with the careful scaffolding by the teacher, that helps students become proficient comprehenders of text. The flow of the lessons can be planned, but often, you will need more texts or more interactions than you had anticipated. The texts are important in that they need to facilitate the depth of thinking that you are trying to teach. Fortunately, there are many, many texts available for your use. Quality literature in picture book and short text formats are far more abundant than they have ever been. Sometimes, a text won't grab your students' engagement as much as you think it will. It is your decision, then, whether the text should be explored more or not. The goal is not learning about the content of the book but about how to comprehend fully and deeply during these lessons. Our experience is that the texts that work best are the ones that students have an emotional reaction or attachment to. We have included an Appendix of possible texts for teachers to use as a starting point (see pages 115–128).

As with all teaching, if there is a school plan or a pacing calendar in place and teachers have collaborated to build a common understanding of vocabulary and teaching interactions, strategic teaching will be much easier and more effective.

In this chapter, we focused on using interactive and shared reading to help our students employ the comprehension strategies to think more deeply about what they are reading. Are these strategies all that our students will need to be strategic readers? No—as you will see in Chapters 3, and 4, our students need to understand and use text types, text structures, and text features to handle the literacy demands of the 21st century.

Chapter 3

Understanding Genre/Text Types Using Interactive Read-Alouds and Shared Reading

Let's Join Val and Her Third Graders as They Begin a Study on Realistic Fiction

Val gathers her third graders on the rug. *Rivka's First Thanksgiving* (Rael, 2001) is up on the electronic camera. "Do you remember this book?" she asks. Most of the students nod; several say, "Yes!" One student immediately responds, "We read this right before Thanksgiving."

"That's right," Val responds. "We did read it before Thanksgiving, and you noticed the kind of questions I was asking as I read the book. I had a lot of questions because this book was so different from the other books we read about Thanksgiving. Today, we're going to revisit this book to notice how the author goes about telling the story."

As she reads and her students follow the text, Val asks, "Who is telling this story?"

At first, students think it might be Rivka, but they soon realize the narrator is not Rivka. Someone who is not in the story is telling it. This leads them to go back to the author's note at the beginning of the book. They find out that this story is based on an experience the author had, but it is not her actual experience.

At this point, one of the students says, "Then it's not a memoir."

Val answers, "You're right, it isn't a memoir. What do you think it is?"

"A story."

"Fiction."

"Maybe its real fiction, like *The Promise Quilt.*"

Val nods. "Good thinking. It is like *The Promise Quilt* (Ransom, 2002). It could be real. Remember, we don't call it real fiction, but realistic fiction. Now, I'm wondering: Does realistic fiction always tell a story?"

This shared reading begins Val's study of narratives, specifically realistic fiction.

> **Wait a minute—did you say shared reading? I thought we always started with an interactive read-aloud.**

Yes, we did say shared reading. In the first two chapters, we spent a lot of time explaining how to start with an interactive read-aloud to introduce the vocabulary and reading behaviors associated with the comprehension strategies. Why has Val started her unit on narratives with a shared reading? When you begin to look at a specific genre or text type, it can be helpful to revisit a favorite book or text you've used previously as an interactive read-aloud. In the interactive read-aloud, you demonstrated the thinking that helped you make meaning of the text. Once you and your students are familiar with that text, you can revisit it in a shared reading to look more closely at the structure or text type. At this point, you have some options: You can begin your genre study with an interactive read-aloud or a shared reading.

Val builds on her students' growing knowledge of how texts work with her choice of *Rivka's First Thanksgiving*. For some units, this may not be feasible. In that case, conduct interactive read-alouds to introduce reading examples of the text type you are introducing to your students. This enables them to begin thinking about this new text type.

> **Text type? Genre study? Are these terms synonymous?**

Genre, text type, mode, register—the more we looked into what we thought was a straightforward matter, the more we discovered that there is little agreement about genre and text type definitions. While we were fascinated by the arguments put forth, as teachers we need a logical explanation that is useful, practical for reading (and writing), and easy to explain to students. This is an important discussion for all districts and schools to have to ensure that the use of the terms *genre* or *text type* becomes uniform. There is no point in making instruction more difficult than it already is for teachers and students.

As we researched, we did find some explanations that make perfect sense to us and we have adopted the definitions of genre and text type from several researchers.

A genre is much more than a 'text type' with a fixed, static, and arbitrary form. Rather, genres have evolved in response to certain social purposes that certain types of writing have to serve; genres come to have textual elements that they do because those textual elements have been found over time to be capable of accomplishing what writers typically need to accomplish with those sorts of texts. Ramona Tang (2006)

To explain these concepts further, the table from the Writing A–Z Web site put it all into perspective for us. We find its clear explanation of genre, as relating to audience and purpose, and text types, as groups of texts that have features of language in common, very useful.

The A–Z table has been written for the purposes of a writing program, so it doesn't include some of the text types we think are important for a reading program. We have added some additional text types for study: Web sites, directions, and game instructions (see Figure 3.1 below). We would also add a genre of poetic writing because to us there is not a category to explain the purpose of poetry and poetic writing.

Figure 3.1

Genre and Text Types

Genre	Text Type/Description
EXPOSITORY	Writing that informs, describes, or explains; text types include autobiography, biography, descriptive, essay, informational reports, and media articles
NARRATIVE	Writing that entertains or tells a story; text types include adventure, fairy tales, fantasy, historical fiction, mystery, personal narrative, realistic fiction, science fiction, folktales, legends, myths, and graphic novels
PERSUASIVE	Writing that attempts to convince readers to embrace a particular point of view; text types include advertisement, editorial, persuasive essay, political cartoon, pro/con, and review
PROCEDURAL	Writing that explains the instructions or directions for completing a task; text types include experiment, how-to's, recipes, directions, and instructions
TRANSACTIONAL	Writing that serves as a communication of ideas and information between individuals; text types include business letter, friendly e-mail, friendly letters, interviews, invitations, postcards, speeches, weblog entries, and Web sites
POETIC	Writing that uses sensory and descriptive language; text types to represent ideas and feelings include haikus, prose, ballads, chants, and songs
HYBRID	Writing that combines genres; text types with multiple purposes that include literary nonfiction

Adapted from WritingA–Z.com, 2009

Hybrid texts—why is this category included?

Literary nonfiction doesn't fit into one category of genre, so we felt our table needed the category of Hybrid Texts. We have modeled lessons using literary nonfiction texts frequently in Chapters 1 and 2, and they are fantastic resources for teaching reading. We particularly love the Read and Wonder books—for example, *The Emperor's Egg* (Jenkins, 2002), *One Tiny Turtle* (Davies, 2005), and *Walk with a Wolf* (Howker, 2002). These books are a combination of the narrative and expository genres woven together to encourage children to wonder at the lives of these animals and to learn facts at the same time.

Hybrid texts probably won't be the last category we will need to add as technology advances our forms of communication to text types we can't even imagine at the moment. Looking at the purpose and audience will allow us to add new genres and new text types in the future.

A word of warning, though—expect to see the terms *genre* and *text type* used interchangeably in many references. One way is not necessarily more correct; the point is that schools and districts need to decide on one explanation and communicate it to all teachers to promote consistency and avoid reteaching.

Now I'm overwhelmed! I have to teach comprehension strategies and genre and text types! How do I do that?

There are many ways to organize your reading curriculum. One way is to pace out the comprehension strategies and include the genres and text types within that teaching. Another way is to build units of study in reading that intersperse genre or text type units with a concentration on reading strategies. Both ways ensure students learn how to use reading strategies and can articulate the features of the text types they read and write.

In Chapter 2, we talked about the "Big Hits" for comprehension strategies. It is equally important for schools to consider the "Big Hits" for text types. Students will be reading a variety of text types in each grade: those they have been exposed to in previous grades, and those they will explore more thoroughly in upcoming grades. The "Big Hits" is not designed to limit the type of texts students will read at each grade level, but rather to ensure they fully understand the features of that text type and they are not revisiting the same text types year after year.

The chart in Figure 3.2 below shows our thinking about the "Big Hits" for each grade level.

Figure 3.2

Genre/Text Types Big Hits

Grade Level	Genre/Text Type
2nd	Simple informational texts
	Fairy tales
	Poetry
3rd	Realistic fiction
	Poetry
	Biography
	Mystery
	Literary nonfiction
4th	Historical fiction
	Web sites
	Graphic novels
	Poetry
	Feature articles
5th	Science fiction
	Fantasy
	Hybrid texts (texts with more than one genre)
	Newspapers/magazines
	Essays

 Let's head back to Val's room to see how she begins a unit on literary nonfiction with an interactive read-aloud.

Val is ready to introduce her students to literary nonfiction. This is a relatively new text type for her students, but one they love. Last year, and earlier this year, Val read some books of this text type to her students, including *Walk with a Wolf, Bat Loves the Night* (Davies, 2004), and *Big Blue Whale* (Davies, 2001). Today, she is going to do an interactive read-aloud with a book with which they are not familiar, *Surprising Sharks* (Davies, 2005). Although the class is familiar with this type of text, Val has not used the term *literary nonfiction* or explicitly taught the features of this text type.

She begins by reading the cover to students. "Does anyone remember any books we've read by this author, or books that remind you of this book?"

One student who loves nonfiction immediately responds that *Bat Loves the Night* is by the same author. Another student thinks there are some Read and Wonder books like this in the school library. She took one out about horses.

Val acknowledges that *Bat Loves the Night* is by Nicola Davies. She also holds up *Big Blue Whale*, and, upon seeing the cover, many students remember hearing the book last year. Val continues, "These books are all a special text type called *literary nonfiction*. I know *nonfiction* means the book is true, but when I think back to *Bat Loves the Night*, I remember there was a story. I am thinking that literary nonfiction will be a story with facts."

Val opens the book and looks at the front end page. "Wow! The author even uses this page to tell us facts. I didn't even know that most of these kinds of sharks existed, and I love the way we can see the size comparisons. I wonder if the author shows a page of facts and then part of the story. That is not what she did in *Bat Loves the Night*, but maybe it's one way to put the facts with the story. Let's see."

As Val reads the book, she points out that it sounds like the author is talking to the reader. It doesn't sound like a story, but there are two different kinds of writing. One kind sounds like a conversation about sharks, and it is displayed in one type of font. The other kind of writing consists of facts and labels. These facts are always in a smaller font.

About one third of the way through the book, Val says, "This could be confusing to read. Do I read all the parts where the author is talking to me first, then read the labels and facts, or should I read all the facts first and then read the other part? So far, I have been reading the part where the author is talking to me first and then the facts. I like reading it this way, so I think I will continue doing that. I am beginning to think literary nonfiction puts two kinds of writing together. It seems like one grabs your attention in some way and the other gives you facts. I wonder if this is true for all literary nonfiction?"

Val continues reading the book. noticing how both parts of the text work together. After finishing the book, she creates a chart of what she thinks is true about literary nonfiction from reading this book (see Figure 3.3 on the next page).

Figure 3.3

Features of Literary Nonfiction

- There is a story. FICTION / REALISTIC

- Facts about the animal or place are off to the side—there is also a note at the end.

- There are pictures, not photos.

- Sometimes, facts are part of the story.

Over the next three weeks, Val will use literary nonfiction with several interactive read-alouds and several shared readings. Each reading will help scaffold students' thinking about literary nonfiction. As the unit progresses, Val and her students see that literary nonfiction consists of two types of writing: one that grabs your attention and one that presents facts. Students will look for this type of writing when they are reading independently. To support some of her struggling students, Val meets with them in a small group and continues to help them understand the features of literary nonfiction and how to navigate the reading when there are two types of text present.

Do I organize my year around comprehension strategies or text types?

Some teachers organize their year around comprehension strategies. Within each unit, they use a variety of text types. They weave the teaching of the text types, text structures (see Chapter 4), and even their content area reading into each comprehension unit. The chart in Figure 3.4 on page 60 shows a year for a third-grade class organized this way. The boldfaced strategy and text type will be the main focus of the unit, with the other strategies and text types woven into it.

Figure 3.4

Pacing Calendar: Based on Comprehension Strategies and Integrating Text Types

Time	Comprehension Strategy	Text Types
about 6 weeks	**monitoring for meaning** and schema (strategy from 2nd grade)	series books, **realistic fiction,** informational texts, news-magazines such as *Scholastic News* or *Time for Kids*, and math texts
about 6 weeks	**asking questions,** monitoring for meaning, schema, and inferring (strategy from 2nd grade)	**mysteries,** realistic fiction, poetry, informational texts, and newsmagazines such as *Scholastic News* or *Time for Kids*
about 6 weeks	**synthesizing,** asking questions, monitoring for meaning, schema, inferring, and determining importance (strategy from 2nd grade)	**literary nonfiction,** realistic fiction, poetry, informational texts, and newsmagazines such as *Scholastic News* or *Time for Kids*
about 6 weeks	**creating mental images,** synthesizing, asking questions, monitoring for meaning, schema, inferring, and determining importance	**poetry,** literary nonfiction, realistic fiction, informational texts, and newsmagazines such as *Scholastic News* or *Time for Kids*
about 8 weeks	work with multiple strategies at once	**biographies,** literary nonfiction, realistic fiction, poetry, informational texts, and newsmagazines such as *Scholastic News* or *Time for Kids*
about 3 weeks	test prep	**various text types that students are expected to respond to on state tests**
about 3 weeks	review multiple text types	multiple text types

Other teachers organize their year around genres and specific text types. Within each unit, they also focus on one strategy and review previously taught strategies. The chart in Figure 3.5 on the next page shows a year for a fourth-grade class organized this way. The boldfaced text type and strategy will be the main focus of the unit, with the other text types and strategies woven into the unit.

BUILDING INDEPENDENT READERS© 2011 by Valorie Falco and Rochelle P. Soloway • Scholastic Teaching Resources

Figure 3.5

Pacing Calendar: Based on Text Types and Integrating Comprehension Strategies

Time	Text Types	Comprehension Strategy
about 4 weeks	various text types, specifically realistic fiction, mysteries, and literary nonfiction, as well as content area textbooks	**monitoring for meaning,** asking questions, synthesizing, creating mental images (strategies from 3rd grade)
about 5 weeks	**graphic novels** and realistic fiction	**inferring** and monitoring for meaning
about 5 weeks	**Web sites,** informational texts, and literary nonfiction	**determining importance,** inferring, and monitoring for meaning
about 6 weeks	**historical fiction**	**schema,** determining importance, inferring, and monitoring for meaning
about 6 weeks	**feature articles**	schema, determining importance, inferring, monitoring for meaning, asking questions, synthesizing, and creating mental images
about 4 weeks	**poetry**	schema, determining importance, inferring, monitoring for meaning, asking questions, synthesizing, and creating mental images
about 3 weeks	test prep	**various text types that students are expected to respond to on state tests**
about 4 weeks	review multiple text types	multiple strategies

After having organized our instruction first around comprehension strategies and then around genre/text types, we now believe it is most effective to alternate between comprehension strategies and genre/text types. This alternation allows teachers to focus their instruction on the area that is most important at the time. Ultimately, our students need to use the comprehension strategies and text types fluidly to fully navigate whatever they are reading. The chart in Figure 3.6 on page 62 shows a year for a fifth-grade class organized in this way.

Figure 3.6

Pacing Calendar: Alternating Comprehension Strategies and Genre/Text Types

Time	Unit of Study
about 3 weeks	**monitoring for meaning** across various texts
about 5 weeks	**science fiction**
about 3 weeks	**inferring** across various texts
about 4 weeks	**newspapers/magazines**
about 3 weeks	**asking questions** across various texts
about 5 weeks	**fantasy**
about 3 weeks	**synthesizing** across various texts
about 4 weeks	**essays**
about 3 weeks	**hybrid texts**
about 3 weeks	**test prep**

Once a district has agreed upon the comprehension strategies and text types to be taught, the organization and pacing of the year can be left up to the teachers. A systematic plan for instruction ensures there is a common language and knowledge base for all students. Teachers are able to choose texts and develop a time frame that reflects the needs of their students.

 ### Let's watch as Rochelle integrates historical fiction into her unit on schema.

Picture books offer a wealth of material for studying historical fiction. The pictures and the relatively short text allow students to learn about different periods of history in a brief amount of time. Historical fiction is also a natural mix with the use of schema or background knowledge to comprehend the text. Without some understanding of the historical context, many stories cannot be understood in any depth.

According to our plans, fourth-grade students have studied the schema comprehension strategy in first and second grades and have used and refined it with third-grade texts the year before. In fourth grade, we are ensuring that the curriculum will be rigorous and not a repeat of earlier years by combining the comprehension strategy with the study of an important text type—historical fiction.

To introduce the study, Rochelle decides to use *The Harmonica* (Johnston, 2008). This is a powerful story of a boy who survives a German concentration camp during World War II by playing harmonica for the commandant. The illustrations are rich and dark, and the language used is expressive and evocative. This book is ideal for students to explore the necessity of using the schema strategy (building background knowledge) to fully comprehend this historical fiction. A picture book allows students to use the illustrative supports to understand the characters' daily lives. In this particular book, the illustrations show readers the fear that the characters feel as the story unfolds. The challenges in the text are learning about the war from the point of view of a Jewish boy and the specialized language referring to the countries and the roles of the people involved. Although this is not a book with many people and place names, proper nouns can often be a challenge in this text type, too.

Rochelle's interactive read-aloud begins like this: "Today, we are going to start reading some historical fiction. You have some experience with this text type already. Remember when we read *Freedom Summer* (Wiles, 2001)? (The class read this story earlier in the year. It is about two boys living in the South when the Civil Rights Act of 1964 was passed.) What do you think you know about historical fiction that would help you read this with understanding? Don't forget to use what you know about fiction as well as historical fiction. Turn and talk to your partner now."

A few minutes of buzz occurs, and Rochelle is able to begin to list the features of historical fiction: it's a story, but it's not all true; it has a beginning, middle, and end; it's about a time in history, like 1964; and it talks about how people used to live.

Rochelle says, "Yes, it is all those things, and today we are going to talk about features that make historical fiction hard to understand sometimes. I am going to read *The Harmonica* and do a think-aloud about what I know about this time period before I read, and about what I am learning about it, during the reading.

"I can see on the front cover a drawing of a young boy in a prison uniform with a number on his shirt, looking sadly at a harmonica. There are rows of barbed wire beside him, and a lot of boys and men behind him. They are all wearing the same uniform and look very thin and unhappy. I can also see a red Star of David on the uniform, so I know that this book is probably set at a prison camp during World War II when all Jews were taken from their homes and put into terrible concentration camps by the Nazis. I have really good background knowledge about this war because I am older and have heard about it throughout my life. There is something I could use to help me, though, if I didn't have any background knowledge. On the inside cover, there is a blurb, and I will read it to you."

The blurb explains that when the Nazis invade Poland, a family is split apart. It goes on to give the outline of the story. Sometimes, Rochelle doesn't want to read this to the students and give away the plot, but her purpose today is different. She wants to show students that there are supports in books that they can use independently.

"Well, I thought the story was set in Germany, but it is also set in Poland," Rochelle observes. "The words *Holocaust survivors* remind me that there are museums and books about people who did survive these camps. Let's find Poland and Germany on our map."

After locating the countries on the map, Rochelle discusses how the countries are next to each other in Europe. They also look at how far the countries are from America. Rochelle explains that she now knows this book is set in about 1939 during a very sad period of history when many countries were fighting one another. To help give students some context, she mentions that she wasn't born then but her parents were.

Then she says, "The more I can figure out about the history before I read, the more I can understand as I read. I want you to listen to how I add to my knowledge from the story as I follow what happens to the little boy on the cover."

Rochelle reads to the page where the family hears Schubert's melodies from their neighbor's gramophone. "I know that melodies are music, so I guess that Schubert was a person who wrote music at the time and a gramophone was like a CD player today. It's interesting when you realize our lives are so different today. I'll read on to confirm and see if my ideas work with the story."

Rochelle demonstrates thoughtful reading, stopping and thinking, making her best guess, and moving on. We want to encourage students to retain the storyline and understand the deeper meanings. Schubert becomes very important in this story. It's his music the boy plays and the commandant loves, and it saves his life. On this first reading, we are thinking of the historical context and the plot. For the second interactive read-aloud, we would move on to discuss the deeper meaning of how the commandant could love beautiful music but still treat so many people so terribly.

As you release responsibility to students, the challenge is always how much to tell them about the time period and how much to leave for them to problem-solve and learn about. If we tell them everything, we leave little work for them to do in unraveling these times. If we tell them too little, they may not understand much at all.

> *You showed a lesson using a text type to help students understand schema. What if I am focusing on a text type and want to integrate a comprehension strategy?*

Let's join Val in a second-grade classroom as she introduces inferring into a unit on fairy tales.

This class has been reading and listening to fairy tales for two weeks. Val has done three interactive read-alouds and two shared readings with traditional fairy tales. Students have a good understanding of this text type.

Val is going to do an interactive read-aloud of *The Three Little Wolves and the Big Bad Pig* (Trivizas, 1997) to introduce students to inferring. The class has been practicing monitoring for meaning and using their schema.

She begins by asking students to name some of their favorite fairy tales. "Little Red Riding Hood," "Goldilocks and the Three Bears," and most of the more commonly known tales are offered.

Val says, "Wow, you all know a lot of fairy tales. I also know you have been using two strategies that help you as readers, monitoring for meaning and using your schema. Today, to help me better understand this story, I am going to be making some inferences. An inference is when I use what is on the page and what is in my head to think about what might happen in the story and why it might happen. I can also make inferences about why a character acts and feels a certain way. I want you to be good detectives and notice when I am doing this kind of thinking."

Val stops on the second page and says, "I don't even have to read the text to know something about the pig. When I look at this picture of his face, I can infer he is one tough pig. A character's expression can help me infer what he or she is thinking or feeling."

She continues to read, stopping several times to make inferences about what might happen next in the story or how a character is feeling. When she gets to the part where the wolves build a house with barbed wire, iron bars, and armor plates, Val says, "This sounds like the part in the story of the three little pigs where they build the house that the wolf couldn't blow down. From the description of the building materials and the picture, I think the wolves will have stopped the big bad pig." She emphasizes her thinking about why she made the inference so students understand that she is using what has happened in the text, as well as what she knows, to make the inference.

Tomorrow, Val will do another interactive read-aloud. This time, she will invite students to make some inferences with her. She will use another fairy tale so students are learning about inferring while expanding their knowledge of fairy tales.

Parting Thoughts . . .

The thinking about genre and text types is not as simple as one might assume. The terms are used one way in bookstores, another in the Library of Congress, and still another in school and public libraries. It is our job as teachers to help students navigate the terms, and more important, the text types they will be required to read or will be interested in reading. We as teachers must become knowledgeable of not just the types of texts we love, or those that appear on a test, but also those our students will face as they become literate citizens of the global community.

Much of the information that our students will need to read and understand will be nonfiction. In the next chapter, we look more closely at the text structures of informational texts. Understanding these structures will allow our students to access information more easily, even information for which they have little or no schema to begin with.

Chapter 4

Teaching Text Structures With Interactive Read-Alouds and Shared Reading

Let's listen as Val does an interactive read-aloud to start a unit on informational texts.

Val begins by writing the heading, "Informational Texts," on a piece of chart paper and asking her third-grade students what they know about informational texts. "You can learn things."

"There are facts in the books."

"It's nonfiction."

"You get information."

Val records their ideas on the chart, commenting that they actually know a lot about informational texts. She then asks why they think she wrote "informational texts" on the chart instead of "informational books."

"Because a text and a book are the same thing."

"Because we are looking at how to use information in a text."

At this point, Val stops and explains that a book is a text but not all texts are books. She displays some articles in magazines and a newspaper and soon students begin to see the difference between a text and a book. One student says, "So you wrote 'Informational Texts' because we are going to get information out of places other than just books."

Throughout this unit, Val will be exposing her students to a variety of texts and text structures. Today, she is doing an interactive-read aloud with a book that has two text structures: chronological and question and answer. Val knows it is important to expose her students to texts and books with multiple text structures early on since it is common for an informational text to have more than one text structure.

"Today I am going to read *Our Seasons* (Lin & McKneally, 2006)," Val tells students. "Before I start, I am going to see what I can learn from the cover and jacket blurb." She reads aloud the brief blurb on the jacket and then says, "From this blurb, I know I am going to learn about the seasons and weather. I notice the author starts the blurb with three questions. I think these questions will probably be answered in the book. The blurb also mentions haiku, which I know is a form of poetry. I know there are many ways to organize information in a text, and I am wondering how the questions and poetry will be used to present the information about the seasons and weather. I think I will begin by skimming through this book to see how it is organized."

As Val begins to skim through the book, she notices three things going on: "Wow, this book is a bit complicated to read. First, I notice the book follows the seasons beginning with autumn, so overall it is in chronological order. The haiku and illustrations complement each other and show something we associate with each season. Lastly, there is a question and then the answer, set to the side on each page. The question is related to something mentioned in the haiku. As a reader, it is helpful if I notice the structure of the text and then make decisions about how I will read it. I think I will read through the haiku first and see what the author is highlighting about each season. I will notice the questions and answers, but I think I will go back and read them after going through the whole book once." Val reads through the book, stopping to observe the connection between each haiku and question. She comments on several questions that pique her interest, noting again that she will go back to read these questions and answers later.

After finishing the book, Val says, "This book has information in the questions and answers, it follows the order of the seasons, and it has a haiku poem on each page about some aspect of the season. There are two structures to this text: one is chronological, and one is question and answer. As we read informational texts, we are going to be looking for the structure the author uses to present information. For each structure, there are words that help us get our brains thinking about the way the information is being presented. In this book, the season words *autumn, winter, spring,* and *summer* are the signal words. We see that a chronological structure follows a certain time order, and a question-and-answer structure starts with a question and then answers it. Tomorrow, we will do more thinking about these two text structures."

With third graders, it is important to use texts with structures that are very obvious. The goal at this level is to create an awareness of the text structures and some of the signal words associated with them. In her next mini-lesson, Val will look at how each question begins in *Our Seasons*. These words and other question words students come up with will be put on a chart of signal words for question-and-answer texts. In addition, while noticing text structures, Val plans to do more shared reading than interactive read-alouds so students are seeing the text and noticing the signal words.

BUILDING INDEPENDENT READERS© 2011 by Valorie Falco and Rochelle P. Soloway • Scholastic Teaching Resources

Text structures? In the last chapter, you talked about text types. How are text structures different from text types?

As we discussed in Chapter 3, text types are the specific types of text found within a genre. The purpose of text types in the narrative genre is to tell a story. These texts all contain the common elements of a story: character, setting, plot, movement through time, and conflict or change. This story structure is carried through the whole text. By and large, this is a structure with which our students are very familiar.

The purpose of text types in the expository genre is to inform, describe, explain, or persuade. A common characteristic of all expository texts is the use of varied text structures that are developed to suit the purpose of the text. A text structure refers to the way an author chooses to organize the information he or she presents. Knowing the common text structures and their related signal words or phrases will help our students predict, confirm, adjust, and determine importance so they are able to understand and ultimately remember the content of the text.

The chart in Figure 4.1 below gives a brief explanation of the most common text structures and the signal words associated with each structure.

Figure 4.1

Nonfiction Text Structures

Term	Signal Words/Phrases
Cause and Effect: Presents facts, events, or ideas that happen as a result of an event. It explains how and why something happened.	• because • since • therefore • if/then, if/can • contribute • cause • thus • as a result • so that • this led to • due to
Problem and Solution: Presents one or more problems and solution(s).	• therefore • if/then • so that • because • dilemma is • problem is • this led to • as a result

Figure 4.1 (continued)

Term	Signal Words/Phrases
Chronological, Sequence, or Time Order: Presents facts or events in the order they occurred. The order may be explicit or implied.	• first • second • third • next • finally • later • before • then • after • now • previously • on (followed by the date)
Description: Presents information about a topic using descriptive details.	• for example • for instance • to illustrate • such as • including • the characteristics
Compare and Contrast: Discusses how two or more ideas, events, people, or things are alike and/or different.	• however • nevertheless • but • similarly • although • yet • otherwise • also • likewise • compared to • either/or • in contrast • in comparison • different • same as
Question and Answer: Presents a question and then provides the answer.	• who • what • where • why • when • how
Enumeration: Presents a list of ideas or steps in a specific order, one after the other.	• 1, 2, 3 • first • second • third • next • last

Although knowing the signal words can help our students negotiate these texts, the real challenge is helping them recognize these text structures when signal words are not present. This is especially true for cause and effect, problem and solution, and compare and contrast. Many texts our students face in the upper grades follow one or more structures but lack the signal words. We need to help them use the signal words to restate information in the text as a way to confirm its structure.

Let's join Rochelle and a class of fourth graders as they look at a text structure without clear signal words.

Most children do well with cause and effect with the simpler texts they are exposed to in first and second grades. As students begin to read about real problems in their world, the cause-and-effect structures in these texts become more complex. Causes and effects often form chains, with an effect becoming a cause. This can become confusing to students who expect a cause to have one or two effects.

Rochelle begins her interactive read-aloud lesson: "Today, we are going to begin to read a book about global warming. What background knowledge do we have about global warming?"

"The Arctic is melting."

"Polar bears might have trouble living if it gets warmer."

Rochelle has scanned part of the text into the computer and has it ready to display on the whiteboard. She shows the students the cover and reads the title, *Get Down to Earth! What You Can Do to Stop Global Warming* (David & Gordon, 2008). Then she says, "Our reading work today is going to be to figure out how the text organizes the causes and effects of global warming. I think understanding the causes and effects of global warming will help us form our own ideas about what we can do to address this issue. Let's read the first page together."

Rochelle reads aloud the first two paragraphs and then tells students, "For this page, I am going to think aloud about how I recognize cause and effect in the text. I am going to use chart paper to make notes of my thinking. I have been thinking about how I am going to organize my thinking. I think I'll create my own graphic organizer. Okay, the first paragraph is easy to understand. The word *so* is in the sentence about getting hot: 'so we kick off the blankets and cool down.'"

Rochelle records that information in a graphic organizer she has created on chart paper.

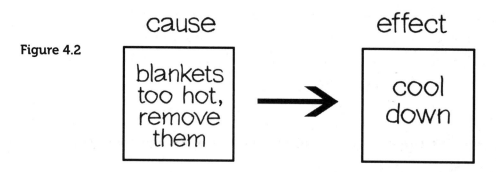

Figure 4.2

"Now, I am going to record what I learned from the second paragraph."

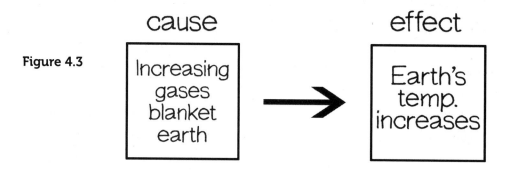

Figure 4.3

Rochelle reads the rest of the page. She invites students to join in the reading if they like. After reading this page, Rochelle says, "Well, we read a lot of information about carbon dioxide: how it is necessary to life on Earth. We read that carbon dioxide, or CO_2, **contributes** to those gases that form the blanket around Earth. *Contributes* is a word that tells us CO_2 is a cause, so I can say Earth is getting hotter (effect) because of the increasing CO_2 (cause). If I can put the information into a sentence with the word *because*, then I know it is a cause and effect."

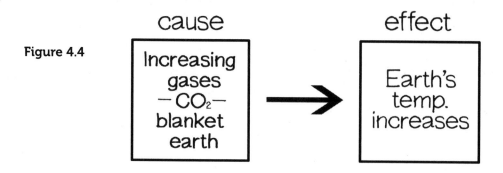

Figure 4.4

BUILDING INDEPENDENT READERS © 2011 by Valorie Falco and Rochelle P. Soloway • Scholastic Teaching Resources

Rochelle and the class read the second page. Then she says, "We read a lot of interesting facts about how carbon dioxide is absorbed into the ocean floor or buried underground. This information helps me think about the next cause and effect. Listen carefully; I am going to reread the part that will contribute to my graphic organizer:

> And over thousands and millions of years, much of this carbon ends up
> buried underground or at the bottom of the oceans.
> *Every living thing on planet Earth is part of the natural carbon cycle.*
>
> This is how it has always worked. But, recently, we have been asking too
> much of the carbon cycle. **Cars, factories, and electric power plants have
> been putting too much of this buried carbon into our atmosphere.**"

(David & Gordon, *Get Down to Earth! What You Can Do to Stop Global Warming*, 2008, p. 5)

Rochelle continues, "If I restate this information, I can say that cars, factories, and power plants release buried carbon, **and as a result**, the CO_2 increases in the atmosphere. I guess that building these factories and plants releases the carbon into the air. I am going to add this information to my graphic organizer because it shows cause and effect relating to the global warming."

Figure 4.5

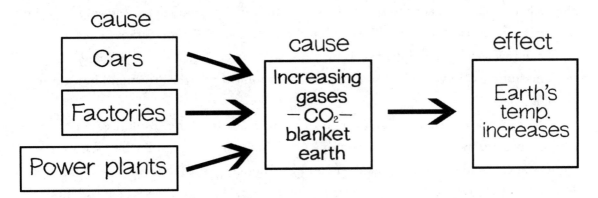

"Wow, this is getting complicated," Rochelle says. "Look how my graphic organizer is changing: When I added the cars, factories, and power plants, the increasing gases became **an effect as well as a cause.**"

As Rochelle and the class continue to read together, they find a section of the text that is clearly using a cause-and-effect structure. The subheading is "If Earth's average temperature increases even a few degrees, gigantic changes can happen."

"This subheading is very helpful to me in looking for cause-and-effect writing," Rochelle points out. "I see it contains *If/can*. I can use these important signal words to say that if Earth's temperature increases, then the following things can happen: The Arctic ice will melt and more floods, droughts, storms, hurricanes, and heat waves will happen. Let me add this to the graphic organizer."

Figure 4.6

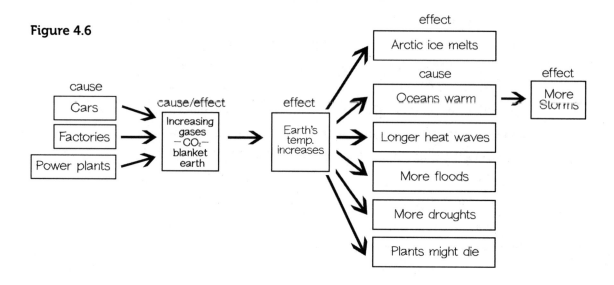

Each lesson lasts about 15 to 20 minutes, and reading and discussing this section of the book takes three days. The short lessons allow students to maintain engagement. As Rochelle reads on, she adds to the graphic organizer in different colors, showing how she is recognizing cause and effect. She explains how she tests the information by restating what she reads using the signal words for cause and effect (e.g., *because, if/then, that led to*). The students are very interested in how the graphic organizer grows and how causes become effects.

The purpose of graphic organizers is to record your thinking. Building your own graphic organizers as you think through a text is important for students to see so they understand how the graphic organizer can help them organize their own thinking. Rochelle selected the type of recording as she thought through the text so students could see how to select and use graphic organizers independently to represent how they think. Too often, students see graphic organizers as boxes to fill in and don't connect them to their real purpose.

Next week, Rochelle and the class will go on to look at *Volcanoes* (Simon, 2006). Students will still participate in shared reading, but Rochelle will make it collaborative, with the students interacting with one another and with her, so they can practice interpreting cause-and-effect structures in text.

> *I am beginning to see the difference between a text structure and text type, but why is it important for our students to know these structures?*

As proficient readers, we integrate our knowledge of how to read specific texts so quickly we often don't realize we are doing it. Think of how you approach reading a newspaper or magazine compared to how you read the instructions for a new piece of technology you are about to use, or a novel by your favorite author. Completely differently!

Students need to begin to think through similar processes. If we help them build metacognitive understanding of what they are doing before, during, and after reading, students can then apply these thinking strategies to texts that are difficult for them. Of course, in our classrooms, we have students who are strategic readers integrating the strategies, students who are using the strategies but are unaware of how they are using them, and some students who are reading just to get through all the words. This last group needs a lot of modeling, many think-alouds, and frequent conferences, so they can learn to think while they are reading.

When students are at a loss to explain or articulate what they are noticing about a text before they read it, an easy way to help them begin to think about it is to ask, "Is this a fairy tale?" when it clearly isn't. Their shocked looks and immediate answers to the negative indicate it's often easier to use a non-example to help students become metacognitive about their thinking. The next questions are "Why isn't it?" and "How do you know?"

For our students to be capable, independent readers, they need to be able to automatically integrate their knowledge of comprehension strategies, text types, and text structures. Some students begin to make these connections on their own, but most need support, through modeling and guided practice, to become strategic readers.

 Let's head back to Rochelle and the fourth graders as they look at the text structure in a text type.

Rochelle and the class have been reading feature articles. Today, they will revisit one of those feature articles, "Paper or Plastic? Neither!" from *Get Down to Earth! What You Can Do to Stop Global Warming*, as a shared reading to look at text structures.

Rochelle puts the article on the electronic camera. The students immediately recognize it. She says, "Here is one of our favorite feature articles. As we've learned, all feature articles have facts plus story and/or strong voice and/or opinion. We can also use our feature articles to learn about text structures. A text structure is the way the author chooses to organize information. Here is a chart with the common text structures and the signal words associated with them."

Rochelle displays an enlarged version of the chart Nonfiction Text Structures (see pages 69–70). After reading through the chart, she says, "Sometimes, there are words in the text to help signal the text structure, but what about when those signal words aren't present? Does this mean there is no text structure? I don't think so, but let's look at several parts of this article and see if we can identify the structure the authors used."

Rochelle draws the students' attention to one of the sidebars in the text, "Corny but True." She reads the first sentence: "Americans buy more than 25 billion single water bottles a year, and, believe it or not, *2.5 million of them get thrown away every hour*." Then she stops and says, "It sounds like this is a problem. The writer doesn't say, 'The problem is', but clearly we can infer that it is a problem. In fact, I could restate this sentence: Americans buy more than 25 billion single water bottles a year, and *the problem is* that 2.5 million of them get thrown away every hour. Once I do this, I predict that there will be a solution to this problem later in this sidebar. Let's see if that is true."

As Rochelle reads the rest of this sidebar, she is able to confirm that there is a solution to the problem. Students see this section clearly has a problem and solution structure, but there are no signal words. By thinking about the signal words and seeing if these words can be used to restate the information in the text, Rochelle and the class are able to understand the structure of the text.

They continue looking at other sections of the feature article, and they come to believe the whole article has a problem-and-solution structure even though there are no clear signal words to help them.

 First, I thought I had to organize my instruction around comprehension strategies. Then you added text types. Now you've added text structures. I'm really not sure how to fit it all in!

As we discussed in Chapter 3, there are multiple ways to organize your reading instruction for the year. If you build your year around comprehension strategies, you could add instruction on specific text structures as they appear in the informational texts and newsmagazines you use throughout the year. Let's revisit the chart from page 60 of Chapter 3 and see how you would add text structures to a year in third grade that you've built around comprehension strategy instruction (see Figure 4.7 below). The boldfaced comprehension strategy, text type, and text structure will be the main focus of the unit, with the other text types, structures, and strategies woven into the unit.

Figure 4.7

Pacing Calendar: Based on Comprehension Strategies and Integrating Text Types and Text Structures

Time	Comprehension Strategy	Text Types and/or Text Structures
about 6 weeks	**monitoring for meaning** and schema (strategy from 2nd grade)	series books, **realistic fiction**, informational texts, and news-magazines such as *Scholastic News* or *Time for Kids* (*Text structures common to informational texts and newsmagazines are description, chronological, compare and contrast, cause and effect, and problem and solution.*)
about 6 weeks	**asking questions**, monitoring for meaning, schema, and inferring (strategy from 2nd grade)	**mysteries**, realistic fiction, poetry, informational texts, and newsmagazines such as *Scholastic News* or *Time for Kids* (*Text structures common to informational texts and newsmagazines are description, chronological, compare and contrast, cause and effect, and problem and solution.*)
about 6 weeks	**synthesizing**, asking questions, monitoring for meaning, schema inferring, and determining importance (strategy from 2nd grade)	**literary nonfiction** (*description*), realistic fiction, poetry, informational texts, and newsmagazines such as *Scholastic News* or *Time for Kids* (*Text structures common to informational texts and newsmagazines are description, chronological, compare and contrast, cause and effect, and problem and solution.*)

Figure 4.7 (continued)

Time	Comprehension Strategy	Text Types and/or Text Structures
about 6 weeks	**creating mental images,** synthesizing, asking questions, monitoring for meaning, schema, inferring, and determining importance	**poetry,** literary nonfiction *(description)*, realistic fiction, informational texts, and newsmagazines such as *Scholastic News* or *Time for Kids* *(Text structures common to informational texts and newsmagazines are description, chronological, compare and contrast, cause and effect, and problem and solution.)*
about 8 weeks	work with multiple strategies at once	**biographies** *(chronological)*, literary nonfiction, realistic fiction, poetry, informational texts, and newsmagazines such as *Scholastic News* or *Time for Kids* *(Text structures common to informational texts and newsmagazines are description, chronological, compare and contrast, cause and effect, and problem and solution.)*
about 3 weeks	test prep	**various text types and text structures that students are expected to respond to on state test**s
about 3 weeks	review multiple strategies	multiple text types

During a test prep unit, you could also incorporate interactive read-alouds and shared reading of nonfiction passages with specific attention to their structures and signal words. An understanding of text structures is especially helpful when students are faced with reading passages about topics for which they have little or no schema or passages that are above their independent reading levels. The text structures help them anticipate what kind of information is being presented, and what kinds of questions they might be asked to answer. The signal words aid students in trying to locate specific information.

Now let's look at the chart from Chapter 3 (page 61) of a fourth-grade curriculum organized around text types (see Figure 4.8 on the next page).

Figure 4.8

Pacing Calendar: Based on Text Types and Text Structures and Integrating Comprehension Strategies

Time	Text Types and/or Text Structures	Comprehension Strategy
about 4 weeks	various text types, specifically **realistic fiction, mysteries,** and **literary nonfiction**, as well as content area textbooks	**monitoring for meaning,** asking questions, synthesizing, creating mental images (strategies from 3rd grade)
about 5 weeks	**graphic novels** and realistic fiction	**inferring** and monitoring for meaning
about 5 weeks	**Web sites** *(varied text structures)*, informational texts, and literary nonfiction	**determining importance,** inferring, and monitoring for meaning
about 6 weeks	**historical fiction** *(chronological, cause and effect)*	**schema,** determining importance, inferring, and monitoring for meaning
about 6 weeks	**feature articles** *(description, compare and contrast, problem and solution)*	schema, determining importance, inferring, monitoring for meaning, asking questions, synthesizing, and creating mental images
about 4 weeks	**poetry**	schema, determining importance, inferring, monitoring for meaning, asking questions, synthesizing, and creating mental images
about 3 weeks	test prep	**various text types that students are expected to respond to on state tests**
about 4 weeks	review multiple text types	multiple strategies

And, finally, there is the option in which comprehension and text type units are woven throughout the year. On page 80, Figure 4.9 shows the chart from Chapter 3 (page 62) for a year in fifth grade with text structures added in.

Figure 4.9

Pacing Calendar: Alternating Comprehension Strategies and Genre/Text Types and Integrating Text Structures

Time	Unit of Study
about 3 weeks	**monitoring for meaning** across various texts and *all text structures (cause and effect, problem and solution, chronological, description, compare and contrast, question and answer, and enumeration)*
about 5 weeks	**science fiction**
about 3 weeks	**inferring** across various texts
about 4 weeks	**newspapers/magazines:** *all nonfiction text structures*
about 3 weeks	**asking questions** across various texts
about 5 weeks	**fantasy**
about 3 weeks	**synthesizing** across various texts
about 4 weeks	**essays**
about 3 weeks	**hybrid texts**
about 3 weeks	**test prep**

However your district, school, or grade level team chooses to organize your year, it is important that there is a systematic plan for teaching the comprehension strategies, text structures, and a wide variety of text types.

> *I see how I might integrate text structures into a unit focusing on nonfiction, but what if I'm in a unit focusing on a comprehension strategy?*

 ## Let's listen to Val and her third graders.

Val and her class have been working on the comprehension strategy creating mental images. At the same time, as part of their social studies curriculum, they have been learning about harvest festivals around the world and have read *We Gather Together: Celebrating the Harvest Season* (Pfeffer, 2006). Today, they are going to revisit this book for shared reading. A chronological text structure is found throughout the book. Val has put up the pages about Pongal, a harvest festival in southern India. These pages describe each day of this four-day festival.

Val begins, "Last week, we read this book and got a lot of information about harvest festivals. Today, we are going to look at several pages on the electronic camera. Our goal is to learn about the text structure of these pages and then to create some mental images that will help us organize the information."

After reading the pages to the class, Val asks what they notice about the way the information on Pongal is organized. One student observes that the author tells what happens on each day of the festival.

Val asks, "Which words helped you see this?"

"They kind of name each day: 'On the first day, On the second day.'"

"Yes, those words signal how the information is being presented. It is in chronological order. Chronological order lists or tells the events in the order in which they happen. It is certainly easier to understand what the festival of Pongal looks like if we think about the important events for each day. Now, I want you to try to make a timeline in your head of Pongal. What would you draw for day one, day two, day three, and day four?"

Several students offer suggestions for each day.

Val says, "So when we have a text structure that is chronological, we can use our mental images to help us create a timeline of the events. We can try to see one event and then the next. How many of you think you could put the important events of Pongal in order?"

Most students feel that they could do this. Val sends them on their way to complete the task independently. She stays in the meeting space with several students who are having a hard time understanding how to put the images in order.

Parting Thoughts . . .

In Chapter 2, Val helped her students see the comprehension strategies as tools in a toolbox. Helping our students understand the text structures of expository writing gives them more tools for their toolbox. Learning to use these tools makes understanding information, especially information for which they have little or no schema, a little easier.

In the next chapter, we are going to use all our tools to understand content area reading. Our students need to be well equipped for these texts because the material may be above their independent reading level and difficult for them to understand. We will also address test taking. The skills and strategies from this and previous chapters will help prepare your students for the standardized tests they will be taking.

Chapter 5

Building Strategies for Content Area Reading and Test-Taking Skills With Interactive Read-Alouds and Shared Reading

Welcome to Val's Classroom

Val and her third graders are about to begin a unit on the solar system; the emphasis in the beginning of the unit will be on the moon. Val knows her students will bring some knowledge and a lot of misconceptions to this topic. Her goal is to build their schema while clarifying the misconceptions.

Val gathers her class on the rug. Each child has a clipboard, a pencil, a colored pencil, and three sticky notes. Talk partners are sitting next to each other. Val asks one set of partners to sit near her. She plans on interacting with this pair as a way of modeling what the students will be doing. Val holds up the book *If You Decide to Go to the Moon* by Faith McNulty (2005) and says, "We're going to start learning about the moon, and I thought this book might get our brains ready to think about what we know, and help us build up our schema for this topic, too. Also, I know we all have misconceptions about the moon, and hopefully, this book will clear some of these up. To start, I want each of you to jot down two or three things you know about the moon on one of your sticky notes. As you write down your ideas, I'll write mine on the chart paper."

As students begin to write, Val stands behind the easel, jotting her thinking on chart paper. She doesn't want her thinking to be visible to students yet, but during the lesson, she will use the chart to model the way she confirms, adds to, and changes her thinking as she acquires information about a topic. After several minutes, Val says, "Madison, Brad, and I are going to be talk partners today. I want you to watch and listen to our conversation so you'll know what to do with your partner." Val puts the chart paper on the other side of the easel so it is visible to all students (see Figure 5.1 below).

Figure 5.1

- Shape changes throughout the month.
- Moon orbits Earth.
- There is no gravity on the moon.

Val continues, "Madison, would you share what you have on your sticky note?"

Madison shares the first thing on her sticky note: "Nothing lived there."

Val stops her and asks Brad, "Did you have that idea on your sticky note?"

"No," he answers.

"Okay, Madison, read your next idea."

Madison reads something very similar to the first idea on Val's chart.

"Madison, you and I wrote down a similar idea," Val says. "On my chart, I wrote that its shape changes throughout the month. You wrote 'the shape changes.'"

Brad pipes up, "I wrote 'it is not always round.'"

Val replies, "Since we all had this idea, we will put a check by it. The check will help us see which ideas we all know." She then turns to the class. "If any of you put an idea similar to this, you can put a check by it."

Many students have a similar idea and put a check by it on their sticky note.

"Now, turn and share your ideas with your partner," Val tells them. "If you both have the same idea, put a check by it. Turn toward me when you're done sharing."

The students talk with their partners and then turn to Val, indicating they are ready.

Val asks, "What are some of the ideas that you and your partner both wrote down?"

Several partners share, and Val adds the information to the chart. Then she says, "We've done a lot of good thinking about what we know about the moon. Let's read this book so our thinking can grow."

Val begins the interactive read-aloud. After reading about half the book, she stops. "This book has me thinking about the moon differently. When I wrote down my ideas, I didn't really think about what it is actually like on the moon's surface. Now I have some new thinking about the moon. Do any of you have new ideas or changes to your thinking?"

Most of the students nod their heads, indicating that they do.

"Now, use your colored pencil and write the new ideas on a new sticky note. If you need to change an idea or add to an idea you have already written down, make the additions and changes with your colored pencil." As the students work, Val adds to her chart.

Figure 5.2

- Shape changes throughout the month.
- Moon orbits Earth.
- There is ~~no~~ less gravity on the moon.
- You weigh less on the moon.
- It's impossible to make a sound on the moon—no air to carry sound waves.
- No clouds to protect from the heat of the sun—things the sun hits → very, very hot.

Several minutes later, students share with their partners, and then several share with the class.

Val says, "I notice we all had new information on our sticky notes and that many of you had to make some changes to your thinking. When we are learning about a topic, we need to think about new ideas and be aware of when our thinking changes."

She continues to read, stopping at the end to once again have students add to and change their thinking about the moon.

> **You said content area reading, but you're not using a textbook. How will using a picture book help my students understand the content at my grade level?**

In Chapter 1, we discussed Ellin Keene's work on essential literacy. The chart on page 10 shows Keene's six essential cognitive strategies, which all readers integrate to construct meaning from text. As readers become more proficient, they use the deeper structures far more than the surface structures. One of the most important deeper structures is the schematic—constructing meaning at the whole-text level and utilizing background knowledge.

This is not new knowledge for any of us. Wilson and Anderson, in their 1986 study, found that having high background knowledge for a topic greatly supports reading on that topic (Duke, 1999, p. 2). A reader's schema or background knowledge is very important to making meaning. In the content areas, teachers expect students to understand many and varied topics. This requires teachers to think about building schema so that all students will be able to access the information required.

> Most 'reading difficulties' are really prior knowledge problems. A few years ago, Illinois administered a statewide test to kids where the topic was in-line skating (rollerblading, to the rest of us). Needless to say, kids from inner-city housing projects knew little about this subject and scored poorly, while kids from wealthy suburbs crisscrossed with recreational trails proved to be 'smarter.' Bah! Some kids just don't have the experience base that makes reading easier for others.
> —Stephanie Harvey and Harvey Daniels, *Comprehension and Collaboration* (2009, p. 22)

Of course, many teachers have experienced the frustration of knowing that their students lack background knowledge and its effect on test scores. Rochelle particularly remembers the discussion and concern that arose about one of the standardized tests after an article on cubism was included. It seemed like none of the students had the background knowledge or schema to answer questions on the subject!

There are many ways for teachers to build schema for their students. Short texts and engaging picture books can clearly provide a bridge to the more sophisticated texts and topics students will be required to comprehend. Ellin Keene reminds us that using these accessible texts that allow students to build schema successfully is critical.

Keene (2008) describes teaching that builds background knowledge as using "way-in texts": "Use way-in texts whenever possible, moving from narrative to expository selections. Way-in texts help to build schema before moving to more didactic text selections; they provide a 'way-in' to understanding more difficult text. They are typically shorter, written in a more narrative style and helpful for building background knowledge for a topic or text structure before students tackle a textbook. . . ." (p. 188)

The explosion of rich, engaging picture books that address many sophisticated topics are the basis of much of our work with students. Throughout this book, we give examples of narrative texts supported by pictures or photographs that allow all students to encounter the ideas in an accessible way.

How do you find books like these? We like to say that we "stalk books in bookshops and libraries." We also read reviews in *The Horn Book*, *The Reading Teacher*, and the *New York Times Book Review*. And as "bookaholics" we are always talking about and sharing books with our colleagues. The Appendix contains a list of some of our current favorite nonfiction and historical fiction books (see pp 121–122). The truth of the matter is that once teachers find the books or short texts that will activate schema, they often put these away. The material is not on the classroom library shelves until after it has been used for the instructional purpose assigned to it. Teachers build a collection of books and short texts over time that can be used to support their curriculum.

Val's class had some schema about the moon, but what about when my students have no schema about a topic?

 Let's join Rochelle as she works with fifth graders. They are learning about the Civil War, but they have little or no schema for the time period or the historical events.

To enter into this study, Rochelle uses *The Silent Witness: A True Story of the Civil War* by Robin Friedman (2008). The story introduces the beginning of the Civil War, moves through a short account of its history, and ends with the surrender of General Lee to General Grant. To engage readers, the author writes the story from the point of view of Lula McLean, the daughter of Wilmer McLean. The McLean plantation becomes the Confederacy's headquarters at the beginning of the war, and their house, in the village named Appomattox

Court House, is where the surrender is signed. Lula has a rag doll her mother made. The rag doll becomes a silent witness to both the beginning of the Civil War and its end. As in many historical books, the names of the people and places are a challenge to navigate as part of the understanding of the account. Students have to understand specialized vocabulary referring to the Union, the Confederacy, and the Civil War to build comprehension. The pictures support the understanding of the daily lives of the people.

Rochelle's interactive read-aloud begins like this: "Today, we are going to read a historical account of the Civil War in a picture book. You have a lot of experience with this text type; for example, remember when we read *The Harmonica* by Tony Johnston? What do you already know about historical accounts that would help you understand this book fully as you read? Turn and talk to your partner."

A few minutes of buzz occurs and Rochelle lists some features of historical texts that students mention, including the following:

"It's a story about a time in history."

"We learn about important events."

"It tells things in the order they happen."

"There are often names of places and people in them."

Rochelle replies, "Yes, all those things are true about historical accounts, and today, we are going to think about what we can do to make historical accounts easier to comprehend. To really understand this book, we need some knowledge of the period of time in which this event takes place. If we have some ideas about what we are going to read, we can add information from this book to our schema. We can also check and see if what we know matches what we read in the book. But if we know nothing about the topic, the other thinking we can use to help us understand this book is our understanding of text structures. Historical accounts are usually in time order. We talked about this recently. What do we know about chronological or time-order texts that could help us understand this book?"

"There might be dates and years."

"The events will be in order."

"We could use sticky notes to record important things that happen."

Rochelle validates these responses and says, "Okay, so now we are ready to think specifically about the Civil War. Take a minute and mentally jot down any ideas you have about the Civil War, and when I signal, share your thinking with your neighbor." While the students are sharing with their partners, Rochelle tries to listen to several conversations.

Then she focuses the students back to the front. "From your conversations, I could tell that some of you know very little about the Civil War, while a few of you know quite a bit. I think it will be helpful to record some of what we think we know about the Civil War on a chart."

Rochelle has quite a few students share and records their ideas on chart paper:

- *George Washington was in it.*
- *I think Molly Pitcher was in it.*
- *Abraham Lincoln was president.*
- *It was between the North and South.*
- *The Underground Railway was part of it.*
- *The North won.*
- *Battle of Gettysburg was the most famous.*
- *It's the only war fought on American ground.*

Then Rochelle says, "We've put down a lot of ideas. It looks like we know quite a bit about the Civil War. Today, I am going to show you how I add information I read to what I know already. I am wondering if this book will start at the beginning of the war and tell me what happened in order. The subheading, 'A True Story of the Civil War,' doesn't give me any clues about when the events in this story take place, but the blurb on the inside cover does. It begins, 'Wilmer McLean could rightfully say, "The war started in my front yard and ended in my front parlor."' From this information, I have decided to write the headings 'Beginning,' 'Middle,' and 'End' on this chart paper. As I read and get new information, I'll record the facts under the most logical heading. I'll read a couple of pages and see if this way of taking notes is working for me."

Rochelle reads four pages aloud to students and shows them the illustrations. "I need to decide what I think is most important from these four pages to write down under my headings. These pages are about the beginning of the war, so I think I will record the date and where the war started because these are important facts about the Civil War." She records the following information under the "Beginning" head:

- *April 12, 1861—first battle*
- *At Fort Sumter, Charleston, South Carolina*

The next page Rochelle reads to the class has important information about the two opposing sides, so she stops and thinks aloud, "I think there is important information on this page. I am going to add facts to the chart about who fought in the war and why." She adds that information to the chart under "Beginning":

- *23 states in North—Union*
- *13 states in South—Confederacy*
- *North—abolished slaves; South—wanted to keep slaves*

Pages 6 and 7 have information about how the Confederacy camped at the McLean plantation at the beginning of the war. Rochelle is conscious that she is stopping after only a few pages, but she is modeling that readers have to stop when they get to important information.

 BUILDING INDEPENDENT READERS© 2011 by Valorie Falco and Rochelle P. Soloway • Scholastic Teaching Resources

She says, "Well, I have only read two more pages, but I think these pages contain important information that I need to record. Sometimes, I read more than a couple of pages before I jot down another note. The number of pages I read depends on where I find the information I am looking for. I am not concentrating on the details about the family because I am reading this book to gather details about the Civil War. I am going to add another fact about the Civil War to the chart." She adds the following fact under the "Beginning" head:

- *July 1861—Confederates camped, McLean Plantation, Manassas, Virginia*

Rochelle continues to read aloud. The next pages add many details about the camp, and she shares that with students, but she doesn't stop to record anything: "The illustrations in this book are giving us a lot of details about life during the war: the soldiers' camp, the clothing, the food, Lula, and her doll. The details in the pictures make me more interested in the book, but today I am looking for facts about the war."

She reads on until she reads a fact about the war: "The part I just read about the first battle of the war is important, and I am going to list it under the 'Beginning' head."

- *First battle—called Battle of Bull Run by the North, Battle of Manassas by the South*

"Now, it's your turn to decide what I should write on the chart," Rochelle continues. "Listen carefully as I read. When I stop, turn and talk to the person next to you and discuss what should be added to the chart."

The students know Rochelle's expectation is that they will turn, face a student next to them, quickly discuss their ideas, and be prepared for her to solicit their thinking. She doesn't use "hands up" because it allows some of her students to not engage and wait for others to answer. It's important for every student to practice this kind of thinking, for it is thinking they will be doing with other documents, stories, and the textbook about the Civil War, and the other content they will study throughout the year.

Rochelle resumes the read-aloud. The text next describes how the Union forces blocked the South's ports from getting staples. Then she stops, and students turn and talk. After a few minutes, she calls on a pair. "Meghan and José, will you tell us what you think we should add to the chart?"

"We think the part about the blocking of the port because that is the part about the war. The other stuff is about the family."

"Who agrees with Meghan and José?" Rochelle asks.

Students indicate by thumbs up or down if they agree. Everyone is in agreement. This is feedback to Rochelle about how her lesson is progressing and whether she has selected the right text for this learning. She has chosen a text that clearly defined the facts about the

Civil War and the information about the McLean family, and students are navigating it well. Rochelle's policy is to initially choose easier texts to help students experience the thinking involved and then move to more difficult texts.

Rochelle also thinks students can build background knowledge about how people lived in the 1860s, especially from the pictures. Later in the unit, she will use the book again to review this type of information.

She addresses the partners, "Everybody agrees with you two, including me, so I am going to record what you said on the chart. I am going to record it under the 'Middle' heading because this information is not about the beginning of the war but about what happened during the war."

- *North blocked South's ports—no staples getting in*

The next day, the class finishes the rest of the book with students interacting with each other and making suggestions about the notes they record. Rochelle continues to record information on the chart, which will be displayed as an anchor chart about the Civil War. Throughout the unit, students will refer back to the chart and add the additional information they learn. The students and Rochelle compare the information they knew before they read the book together and what they have recorded on the chart.

Rochelle ends the lesson: "We now know a lot more about the Civil War after listening to this book and recording facts. I am going to display this chart to represent our schema at this time. As we read our textbook, some primary sources, and other informational texts, I am sure we will add to this chart."

Rochelle's next step will be to pass more responsibility to students during a shared reading of another text about the war.

So if I use an interactive read-aloud to front-load my students, do I still need to do shared reading?

 Yes, we want to gradually release the responsibility to our students. Let's head back to Val's room.

Val begins a shared reading on the moon with students: "Several days ago, we read *If You Decide to Go to the Moon* and then we worked together to create this chart from our sticky notes (see Figure 5.3 on page 91)."

Figure 5.3

- Shape changes throughout the month.
- Moon orbits Earth.
- There is ~~no~~ less gravity on the moon.
- You weigh less on the moon.
- It's impossible to make a sound on the moon—no air to carry sound waves.
- No clouds to protect from the heat of the sun—things the sun hits ➔ very, very hot.
- Ground is covered with rocks and craters.
- Everything is lifeless and still.

"This chart is going to anchor our thinking for our study of the moon. We will work together to confirm the information on it and to add to or change the information throughout the unit."

Val puts an article from the *Science News for Kids* Web site entitled "Not Bone-Dry After All: The Moon Holds Water" on the electronic camera. The title and the two pictures at the beginning of the article are visible to students, as well as the peripheral icons, advertisements, and links to other topics on the site. Val reads the title and the captions and says, "Just looking at the pictures and reading the title and captions gets me thinking that this article is going to be very different from the book we read. What are you noticing?"

"There is something about glue."

"There is a question and places to bubble in an answer."

"There are icons that show you other places you can go."

"There are real photos."

Val quickly realizes that her students are noticing the features of the Web site, not the article. Because her students are familiar with the Internet, she assumed that they understood how a Web site was set up and were able to block out the features unrelated to the article. "You have noticed a lot about this Web site," she says. "Let's look at all the information around the article."

She uses the curser to point to each area around the article. As she points to each one, she asks, "Is this connected to our article or is it a feature of the Web site?" Soon, students see that the "stuff" around the Web site is not part of the article.

Val says, "So, as readers, we have just made a big discovery about reading information on a Web site. You need to be aware of how the site is set up, and when you find an article on a topic you want to read, you need to focus on the article, not the other things on the Web site."

"That's hard because I would want to play the games," says one student.

"Yes, it is hard," Val acknowledges. "We will have to work a bit harder to stay focused. Now, let's bring our attention to the article."

Val displays the body of the article. "I am going to read this to you, and I would like you to follow along."

She reads the first paragraph. After reading, she points out how the article begins: "This just in: There's water on the moon."

Then Val begins to think aloud: "I wonder why the article doesn't just begin with 'There's water on the moon'?"

"Maybe they want you to know it just happened?"

"They want you to know just how it happened."

Although Val's students have spent a lot of time reading pieces with voice and thinking about how an author uses voice to engage the reader, they don't immediately recognize it at the beginning of this piece.

Val says, "I think the author might have chosen to start this way to get us interested in reading the article. I think he wants to signal us that we are going to be reading some new information, but it didn't just happen. So what is the new information?"

"Scientists suspect something."

"You're right, it does say 'Scientists have suspected as much for several years,' but this is not the new information. Can we read this part again and listen for the new information?"

Val rereads the first paragraph, and it takes quite a bit of prompting and guiding for her students to understand that the new information is about there being very small amounts of water all over the moon, not just icy patches at the poles. She continues reading the next two paragraphs and notices that students are really struggling to understand the article. She stops and says, "I am noticing that we are having a hard time understanding this article."

"Yeah, they're doing a lot of talking."

"There are a lot of words."

Val looked carefully at this article before presenting it to her students. She thought that as long as she was reading aloud the article and working with students to construct meaning, they would be able to understand and synthesize the new information. Something is holding them back. Their body language tells Val that they aren't engaged, and yet she knows they are excited with learning about the moon. What is missing?

Val consults her students: "We are having a hard time understanding this article, and although the author tried hard to engage readers, most of you don't seem interested. What are you thinking?"

"I think the words are too close. It looks hard to read."

"I can't tell who's talking. I think it's the author, but then there is a poet. Is the poet a scientist?"

After listening to a few more comments, Val puts the computer to the side and puts an article they read in *ASK* magazine on the electronic camera. She tells students: "This is a long article with a lot of information, and yet we enjoyed reading it. We learned a lot about how moons are made. Why is this so much easier to read?"

"There are cool pictures. You know, those trading card pictures."

"There are headings."

Val comments, "Oh . . . so the text features help you?"

"Yeah, the headings seemed to help break things up."

"I like pictures. They really do get me thinking about things."

Val's students have had two years of reading newsmagazines, such as *Scholastic News* and *Time for Kids*. As third graders, they have spent a lot of time using the text features in these magazines before they begin reading as well as while they are reading. Consequently, Val did what many teachers do—she assumed if she was reading the information in a shared reading, her students would be able to work with her to comprehend the information. The students quickly showed Val that they needed more support. In Chapter 1, we talked about Jeff Wilhelm's gradual release model. In his model, shared reading is "I do, you help." As we saw in this lesson, Val was doing all the work. She realized that she needed to do more shared reading with articles that had a variety of text features so her students had the scaffolding they needed to participate in the shared reading.

> ## Text features? Do you mean the text structures you talked about in Chapter 4 or are text features something different?

We keep text structures and text features clear in our minds with the following:

❖ Text structures are the internal organization of the text, the way the author chooses to present the information, such as cause and effect.

❖ Text features are additions to the running text, such as maps, captions, and photographs.

While our students may not easily recognize the structure of the text, the text features tend to be what draws their attention. A comprehensive understanding of the purposes of text features and the information they convey is an important part of the deeper comprehension of informational texts.

Margaret Mooney (Hoyt, Mooney, & Parkes, 2003) says, "Some of the key understandings in informational texts include the purposes and formats of the title, table of contents, blurb, index, glossary, diagrams, and tables (p. 38)." She expands further by listing the multiple reasons authors might choose to use text features. Here's what Mooney writes about captions:

Captions

a comment under, above, or near an illustration that:

- explains the content or choice of the illustration
- summarizes part or all of the text
- draws the reader's attention to key information
- provides an example of a point made in the text
- presents another point of view
- anchors the text in reality
- expands the reader's view of the text (p. 38)

The multiple purposes of captions indicate that as students grow as readers and the texts they read become more sophisticated, it is not enough for them to be able to identify captions only. They need to recognize a caption's different purposes to gain full information from it.

As we examine the text features that are the most useful to readers, we explore the features that "pop out" to our students, including the following:

- **Photographs:** Many nonfiction texts have lots of photographs of the topic. For many of our learners, using the photographs to add to their understanding is a way to build background knowledge before they read.

  Maps: They are often colorful and essential to building information before, during, and after reading. However, our anecdotal experiences are that students don't look carefully at maps (often they look only at the key), and miss much of the information they can add to their schema. For this reason, we have actually done a series of interactive read-alouds and shared reading using atlases.

A chart adapted from Hoyt et al. and Bluestein (2010) (see Figure 5.4 on the next page) elaborates on the purposes of captions and other text features.

Figure 5.4

Text Feature	Purpose
Table of Contents	• Shows how information is organized • Indicates where emphasis of the book is and number of page numbers in each section • Helps locate specific information • Reveals what the author determined was important about the topic
Headings and Subheadings	• Show what the section or subsection is mostly about • Indicate location of specific information
Index	• Indicates location of smaller sections of the text • Provides easy access to interesting or very specific information • Reveals what the author determined was important about the topic
Glossary	• Explains specific words or phrases in the context in which they have been used by the author • Lists technical words often related only to topic • Gives quick access to meaning of words or phrases
Boldfaced Words	• Highlight words important to the construction of meaning • Highlight words to build background knowledge • Are usually defined in glossary
Diagrams	• Can add details to text • Allow visualization of text • Can simplify the text description • Indicate order • Can add information photographs cannot: cross-sections, details on parts, and so on
Blurbs	• Add important details to the title • Build background knowledge • Persuade readers to read the text • Provide questions that will be answered in the text

Adapted from Hoyt, Mooney, & Park (2003) and Bluestein (2010)

Students are often attracted to the more obvious text features, but to truly use these features to deepen understanding and build schema, they need a lot of guided practice to look carefully at all text features, including those where the information is complex, such as maps, graphs, charts, and tables.

 Let's go back to Val's room. She taught a mini-lesson to get students thinking about text features. Now, she will lead a shared reading of an article and a discussion of its text features.

Val begins by saying: "When we are reading *Time for Kids*, what is the first thing you usually do? Turn and talk to your partner, and see if both of you do the same thing before you begin reading."

After a few minutes, she asks several partners to share.

"We both look at all the pictures first."

"I read the headings, but my partner looks at the pictures."

"I always go to 'The Top Five' article first. My partner likes to look at and read the pictures."

Then Val asks students who read the captions for the pictures first to raise their hands. Over half raise their hands.

"Who starts with the headings?" she asks. About one third raise their hands.

Val continues, "It looks like most of you begin with the pictures or the headings. Before I hand out *Time for Kids*, I often get you thinking about the topics by writing the headings down and having you predict what we will be reading about. This activity gets your brains engaged with the topic. We usually find that some of you know something about the topic and some of you don't. Either way, as a community, we begin to build schema for what we are going to be reading. When we are reading informational texts—books, articles in a magazine, articles online, articles in a newspaper, or instructions for a science experiment—we can use the text features in the same way, to help us begin to think about and then make predictions about the topic. I thought it might be helpful if we made a chart of the text features we have been using and how they help us."

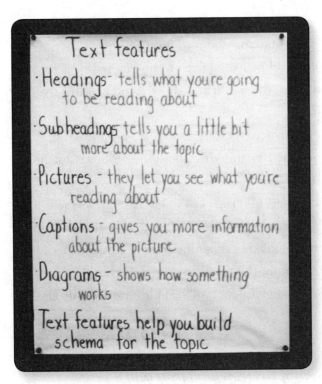

This is the chart that Val and her class created.

After Val and her students have completed the chart, Val says, "Tomorrow, we are going to read another article about the moon. Although it is a long article, I think we will be much more successful in reading it than we were with the article from the science Web site. Tomorrow's article has a lot of text features that will help us comprehend the text."

The next day Val's students gather on the rug. Each has a clipboard, pencil, and several sticky notes. The article "Home Sweet Home" from *ASK* magazine is displayed on the electronic camera, but only the title and subheading are visible to students.

Val begins the lesson: "Today, I am going to start by reading the headings and subheadings in this article to you. As I am reading, I want you to start thinking about what we might learn from this article." After reading all the headings to students, she says, "Talk with your partner and write down on one or two of your sticky notes what we might learn about in this article."

Minutes later, Val has some of the partners share their thinking and then responds: "Wow, you all have a lot of good ideas about what we might learn as we read this article. Let's add to our thinking by looking at the pictures and photographs and reading the captions. Also, speech bubbles are part of many of the pictures. We will need to see how and why the authors use these."

As Val and the class look at the pictures and read the captions, they discuss what other information might be in this article. Many questions arise concerning the vehicles in the pictures. No one has thought about transportation on the moon before seeing the pictures. They also discuss whether the speech bubbles in the photos are helpful or a distraction. Val says, "The headings got us thinking about what we might learn in this article, but did you notice what happened when we started reading the pictures?"

"We had a lot of questions."

"The questions in the speech bubbles got us talking about things."

"I could actually start picturing what it would be like to live on the moon."

"We had to think about what we know about the moon and think if some of this stuff made sense."

Val adds, "We haven't read the text of this article yet, but already we are thinking deeply about the information and how it adds to our thinking about the moon. We seem to have a lot of questions that we're hoping the article will answer."

Now, it's time for Val to read aloud the article, and the class follows along. There is a lively give-and-take between Val and her students as they add to and change their thinking about the moon. Val is able to turn much of the making meaning over to students because of the scaffolding the text features provided before they read the article. From the resulting discussion, she knows there is a lot of information students will be able to add to the class chart about the moon.

This all sounds great, but I must use a textbook. How will understanding text features help my students understand the textbook?

 Rochelle started by building students' schema and understanding of text features with interactive read-alouds and shared reading. Now, she will use shared reading with the textbook.

To enable the fifth graders to gain more in-depth schema about the Civil War, the next lesson Rochelle does uses the social studies textbook. Her objective in this lesson is to look at text on one topic that has multiple text features and to have students integrate the information from each text feature. Textbooks are particularly dense with information presented in multiple ways. The fifth-grade students need to be able to navigate these types of texts so they can learn content from many different resources. Using the electronic camera to enlarge two pages of the textbook, Rochelle asks students to skim the text to see which text features the author uses to give readers information. Students were well versed in text features and skimming before they began this lesson.

Rochelle lists their answers on the whiteboard:

- *Photograph with a caption*
- *Drawing with a caption*
- *Writing in paragraphs*
- *A graph*
- *Questions with a check beside them*
- *Headings in red*
- *An information box about a person*

Rochelle praises students and continues: "Great job, everybody. Look at the chart that we developed several days ago when we read *The Silent Witness: A True Story of the Civil War*. We found that one reason for the war was slavery. Look under 'Beginning': 'North—abolished slaves; South—wanted to keep slaves.' The textbook has information about slavery, and we can read it to learn more about why slavery was such a major reason for the war. When we use a textbook, we are often looking for specific information. We can use the text features to locate the section we need. Which text features on these pages would help us find out more information on slavery?"

"The heading 'The Slave Economy.'"

"The graph. Its heading is 'Southern Slaveholders, 1860' so that must tell us more about slaves."

"The drawing has slaves in it."

Rochelle nods. "Really excellent observations. So we have a drawing with a caption, a heading with some writing, and a pie graph with information about slavery. Which one should we read first?" Then she wonders aloud which text feature students would select to read first.

The class buzzes with disagreement.

"The drawing."

"No, we should start with the writing under that heading. It says 'The Slave Economy' so that has to be more important."

"What about the graph? It tells us stuff about Southern slaveholders, too."

Rochelle refocuses students' attention. "All right, everyone, let's talk about it. Remember that you can read text features in any order because it's gaining the information that's important. How about we start with the drawing and the caption?"

Most of the students agree so they begin to examine the drawing. Rochelle reads aloud the caption and invites everyone to join in the reading. The students have brought clipboards, pencils, and paper to the meeting area to record information. Rochelle asks students to record what they learned from this text feature and she encourages them to write what they have learned in their own words. She also directs students to write about what they learned about slaves and not just what the caption said. Students share their learning with another student near them.

"We know the slaves worked in cotton plantations in the South, because the drawing has slaves working, and the caption says it's a plantation in the South," shares one pair.

Rochelle adds this to their chart under the "Beginning" column.

- *April 12, 1861—first battle*
- *At Fort Sumter, Charleston, South Carolina*
- *23 states in North—Union*
- *13 states in South—Confederacy*
- *North—abolished slaves; South—wanted to keep slaves*
- *July 1861—Confederates camped, McLean Plantation, Manassas, Virginia*
- *First battle—called Battle of Bull Run by North, Battle of Manassas by the South*
- *Slaves worked on cotton plantations in the South*

Then Rochelle tells the class: "Let's read the paragraphs under the heading and see what new information we can learn." After reading the section with Rochelle, students record the new information and Rochelle adds it to their chart. The pie graph is the next text feature to read and interpret, and there is much discussion on what information it gives. The students, with Rochelle facilitating, agree to add this information to the "Beginning" column: Most people in the South did not own slaves: 25% of the people did.

Then Rochelle says, "Let's talk about how we used all three pieces of information to add to our schema on the chart. The next time we need information we can remember these strategies and use them again. Who would like to talk about how we did it?"

"We selected one to start with."

Rochelle continues to prompt students. They are not sure what else to add, and this is the learning that she particularly wants them to take away from the lesson. "What else did we do to understand the information that we added to the chart?" she asks.

"We read one text feature at a time."

"Yes, and we wrote things down on our paper after we read them."

"We had to use our own words."

"Remember why we use our own words?" Rochelle prompts them.

"No plagiarizing!"

"Yes, absolutely," Rochelle agrees, "and also, when you put it in your own words, you really understand what you have read. If you copy the author's words, your brain is not doing the thinking, the author's brain is. Let's go over the process we used to really get the most from the three text features. We read one at a time, wrote notes in our own words, and decided what to add to the chart. We also used all the parts of the text that could help us. Next time you need to find out information, you can use this process to take your notes. Don't forget that information is not only in the writing, but, like today, it can also be in the drawing, graph, photograph, and all the other text features we listed."

Rochelle has used an older textbook for her shared reading. This helped her front-load the concepts, and her next step is to have students read the page in their textbooks that refers to the Civil War.

"During social studies later on today, you and your partner will get your textbook out, read page 57, and take your own notes of any more information we can add to our chart."

At that time, Rochelle conferences with partners and assists where she can see it is necessary. Her plans for tomorrow are to read *Pink and Say* by Patricia Polacco (1994) as an interactive read-aloud. This moving story will help students build empathy for the young soldiers who fought in the war.

If Rochelle is eventually going to have students work in their textbook, why didn't she have them use it for the shared reading?

If each student has a textbook, the temptation to look at other pages rather than where the instruction is taking place is too great. Too often, you will be involved in policing students and not engaging them. Whiteboards, electronic cameras, and overhead projectors allow you to enlarge pages of textbooks so important learning can be ensured. Also, having students working together at a meeting area is really important. Students sitting at their desks are often too far from the teaching and the enlarged text. The opportunities to become distracted are too many.

You have many options in arranging this meeting area: A rug in the center with benches or chairs around the outside is usually more acceptable to older students than just the rug alone. Another option is to have students in desks close to the text stay seated and bring the other students to the floor. Having students within your proximity enables more effective monitoring.

Being part of a group constructing meaning together is powerful because it allows interactive thinking among students, and not just with you. Students prepare their thoughts in pairs (or small groups) and everyone is expected to answer when called upon. Thinking is developed during the discussion before students are expected to begin written responses relating to the content.

I see how I can use high-quality picture books and short texts to build my students' knowledge of a topic. I understand that text structures and text features will help my students read and understand informational texts, including their textbooks, but I have A LOT of material to cover in a year. How can I cover everything I am expected to teach?

Many teachers who are required to use commercial literature anthologies and content textbooks are frustrated because not all students can read them. A frequent solution is for the teacher to read the stories or nonfiction texts aloud. From time to time, the teacher asks some questions from the teacher's manual, but opportunities for responsive teaching, thinking aloud, and talking about the material are few and far between. Most important, the teacher often has no idea whether or not all students understand the text. Following along in a text does not mean a student is understanding it.

Val conducts an interactive read-aloud.

"Using the same literature selection or textbook as a shared read-aloud provides far more opportunities for relevant teaching, focused talk, and student engagement." Regie Routman, (2008, p. 65)

The interactive read-aloud and shared reading lessons described in this book are teaching strategies you can use to cover many important topics. Students are expected to develop a depth of understanding. Textbooks become a resource. Learning from textbooks is a skill that teachers should demonstrate to students frequently. The notion of reading nonfiction to gain information is at the forefront of lessons, as in the Civil War lessons with Rochelle and in Val's lessons on reading about the moon that we've presented in this chapter.

Beginning the thinking around the topic with short texts, such as picture books and excerpts from educational magazines, before moving on to using the textbook ensures that students are prepared to navigate textbooks for their learning. You read the text aloud, think aloud, and invite choral reading and have students turn and talk, think-pair-share, and take short notes to develop engagement, specific vocabulary, and schema. You hold high expectations for all students involved in these lessons.

Jeffrey Wilhelm (2007) says, "The teachers with whom I work seem to grasp intuitively the power of the inquiry approach, but they often resist because, as they say, 'I just don't have the time— there is so much content to cover!' Wiggins & McTighe (2006) argue that this kind of statement confuses information and knowledge, and confuses superficial coverage with the 'uncoverage' of true understandings of how data is structured, and how and why knowledge structures work." (p. 161)

I was thinking, could I use interactive read-alouds and shared reading to help my students with math?

 Absolutely! Let's join Val as she does an interactive read-aloud during math with her second graders.

Val is working to help build her students' sense of numbers. When reading a number sentence such as $4 + 7 = 11$, her students correctly say, "Four plus seven equals eleven." However, when they see the problem $4 + 7 = 8 + \underline{\hspace{1cm}}$, they cannot understand how you can have an addition (or a subtraction problem) after the equal sign. After questioning her students, Val realizes that they don't really understand what *equals* means. As one student puts it, "When I see an equal sign, I know I have to put an answer."

Val knows her students need to build a better understanding of equality before they go any further, so she has decided to do an interactive read-aloud with the book *Equal Shmequal: A Math Adventure* by Virginia Kroll (2005).

Students gather on the rug. Val holds up the book: "This book is titled *Equal Shmequal: A Math Adventure.* It was written by Virginia Kroll. I was thinking that this book might help us get a better picture in our heads of what *equals* means. When you see a problem like the one

I've written on the board, $5 + 9 =$ _____, what do you expect to go in the blank?"

"The answer."

"Is there more than one answer?" Val asks. She calls on several students, and the consensus is that there is only one answer. "It sounds like you all agree on what the equal sign in a problem means, but I am thinking that this book might tell us other ways to think about *equal*. Let's see." Val opens to the title page and says, "Mmm, this picture shows two bees, and it looks like they are playing tug-of-war. One bee seems to be pulling really hard, but I don't think the other bee is putting much effort into it. Luckily, there is the same number of bees on each side, so the contest will be fair." She then reads the next few pages, which show children at a park. They decide to play tug-of-war. A mouse is watching, and once the children leave, the mouse asks a bear to play the game that he has watched the children play.

Val stops and says, "Look, the bear has one end of the rope, and the mouse has the other. The bear gives a yank and easily wins the game. The mouse complains that the teams need to be equal. On the page before, when the children were playing, there were four on each team, but one team won. Now, there is one on each team, and the bear easily won. In both cases the teams had equal numbers, but I don't think they were equal or one team would not have won. I think I'll keep reading. Maybe there are other ways to think about *equal*."

She resumes reading aloud. More animals come and ask if they may play. The mouse says yes, as long as each team is equal. When the bear hears the mouse, he says, "Equal, shmequal."

Val comments, "I don't think the bear cares much about the teams being equal. But the turtle asks, 'What does equal mean, anyway?' Maybe all the animals will work together to come up with an idea about what *equal* means."

Val continues to read, stopping to comment on the ideas that the animals come up with. As she is reading, she can see students are expanding their view of *equal*, just as the animals do. Val turns to the last page in the book: "Look, this page is not part of the story; it tells what it means to be equal." She reads all the explanations of equal and then says, "After reading the story and reading this end page, I notice that *equal* has to do with 'the same.' Look, each example has the words *the same*. And back in the story, when the animals were on the seesaw, the bear was on one side and all the other animals were on the other side. The picture showed a greater number of animals on one side, but the weight of the animals on each side was the same. Maybe if I try to picture things being the same on each side of an equals sign, it will help. I think the picture of the seesaw is a good way to visualize what *equal* means. Tomorrow, when we do problems such as $3 + 4 = 6 +$ _____, maybe that picture of the seesaw will help us."

Parting Thoughts . . .

Throughout this book, we have been adding to our students' toolboxes, giving them tools for reading a wide variety of texts and to recognize the importance of text features. The lessons seem to be going well, but how do we know that our students are using the strategies independently? How do we know that our students understand the topic?

You receive instant feedback from student responses and can adjust a lesson quickly if students are assimilating the new learning quickly or slow down if the opposite is apparent. Reading strategies can be integrated into the content so students' deeper learning of topics is related to how to successfully read content texts. You are also able to facilitate students to focus in on the important ideas and avoid trivial information that would distract them. You model open-ended questions, and pairs of students discuss them. Students are prepared so they can read the relevant section of the text individually or in partnerships.

In the next chapter, we more fully address feedback and formative assessment.

Chapter 6

Assessment on the Go:
Using Interactive Read-Alouds and
Shared Reading for Day-to-Day Assessment

Let's talk about how to assess all your students.

Interactive read-alouds and shared reading offer unique opportunities to understand where students are in their thinking. Their responses, and the conversations you overhear during turn and talk, allow you to develop valuable insights into the invisible deeper structures that we discussed in Chapter 1 on page 10: schematic, semantic, and pragmatic. The assessment we do during interactive and shared reading is not intended to be an assessment of individual students; it gives us feedback on where the majority of students are in their thinking. We are looking at the twists and turns that our learners take as they move to use the strategies and skills independently. This formative assessment provides immediate feedback, so you can adjust a lesson midstream if you think it is necessary.

As you recall, in Chapter 1, Rochelle used a piece about maggots called "Gross but Good." Her instructional focus was on building schema when a reader doesn't know much about a topic. She expected students to know very little about maggots, but when she asked whether anyone knew anything about them, one student described maggots in detail. Rochelle adjusted her next teaching move because the student had explained to the class the necessary details about maggots. That allowed her to move quickly into building students' schema on the medical benefits of maggots, something that was new to all the students.

Assessing deeper comprehension strategies is a challenge. It requires some individual conferring to really assess in the deeper manner that is necessary to advance each student's ability to think about text effectively. The responses and conversations that students engage in during whole-group lessons can allow you to make instructional decisions for your next lesson. They allow you to ask yourself questions such as these:

- *Are students easily understanding the strategies I'm teaching them?*
- *Are they using the vocabulary of the strategy they are learning?*
- *Are they able to explain their thinking in their own words?*
- *Do they need more practice or more modeling?*

Your observations as each lesson progresses will allow you to make very brief anecdotal notes at the end of the session that will inform your next lesson. You can use one or two sentences to remind yourself whether to use the language more explicitly, explain the language more carefully, use more modeling or partner practice, or adjust partnerships between students to encourage more participation or understanding. The notes you jot will help you decide upon the questions you can use during your individual conferences and small-group work. These notes can also influence your choice of text and whether you will do another interactive read-aloud or move to shared reading.

Both of us have shared lessons throughout the book that didn't work; we had to backtrack and find another text. For example, in Chapter 2, when Rochelle taught monitoring for meaning to fourth-grade students, she quickly realized that the language in *Dear Mrs. LaRue: Letters From Obedience School* was too sophisticated for students at that time. It is difficult to monitor for meaning when the reader hasn't constructed meaning in the first place.

Val's use of a Web site to motivate and build her students' schema about the moon in Chapter 5 was similarly unsuccessful. The Web site displayed many peripheral icons with a lot of visual information that distracted students. When Val read the article from the Web site about the moon in a shared reading, students had difficulty because of the density of the text and the lack of photographs and other text features. She discarded this text and chose another text that would suit her purpose equally well. Now, when Val evaluates a Web site to use with her students, she looks closely at the text features available to support her students. When you allow students time and opportunities to think at a deeper level, the choice of text is critical.

 Conversations are important and can provide an excellent window into assessing students' thinking during the interactive read-aloud or shared reading.

When students are talking to one another, in pairs or in groups, you can choose to quickly drop in and listen to a few discussions. This allows you to jot down observations while scaffolding for those students who might need more support or confirming the thinking of students who are moving toward independence. The valuable information that you get from these interactions becomes the formative assessment that enables you to decide, at that moment, whether you can continue with your planned instructional focus or whether you must make adjustments. It can also provide information that you can use to differentiate instruction when you're meeting with small groups or conducting individual reading conferences.

What are we listening for?

We've all heard those students who can use the vocabulary, but don't really go beyond "talking the talk." They parrot the terms—"I'm using my schema, I'm getting a mental image"—but when asked to explain their thinking, their answers are thin. They can't tell why or how their thinking developed. They frequently quote a sentence from the text, but they don't use it to draw a conclusion, form an opinion, make an inference, or actually synthesize the information. As we listen to our students carefully, we consider how their answers reflect their abilities to think and reason deeply.

Stephanie Harvey and Anne Goudvis, in *Strategies That Work* (2000), use the work of Perkins and Swartz (1992) to discuss the four kinds of learners/readers:

❖ *Tacit learners/readers:* These are readers who lack awareness of how they think when they read.

❖ *Aware learners/readers:* These are readers who realize when meaning has broken down or confusion has set in but who may not have sufficient strategies for fixing the problem.

❖ *Strategic learners/readers:* These are readers who use the thinking and comprehension strategies to enhance understanding and acquire knowledge. They are able to monitor and repair meaning when it is disrupted.

❖ *Reflective learners/readers:* These are readers who are strategic about their thinking and are able to apply strategies flexibly depending on their goals or purposes for reading. According to Perkins and Swartz, they also "reflect on their thinking and ponder and revise their use of strategies." (Harvey & Goudvis, p. 17)

Having the patience to listen to our students, to use wait time to allow them to formulate their thoughts, and to use strategic prompts are important teaching moves as we encourage them to progress along the continuum from tacit to aware to strategic readers, finally arriving at truly reflective responses. We would like our students to be reflective learners who use their own language to clarify confusions or misconceptions. They need to be proactive in their construction of meaning, and have an "aha!" moment that motivates them to enthusiastically want to respond to text.

A wonderful example of a reflective response comes in Val's lesson on mental images in Chapter 2 (see pages 44–45). When she asks students what the author did to help them create mental images and why these images helped them as readers, a student sums it up by saying, "When I am standing there right next to the character, it's not just the picture that helps me, but the way the picture makes me feel. I am sucked into being on the adventure with the character, wondering what will happen next." We won't always get these reflective responses, but it is what our teacher radar is listening for.

Sticky notes and other written response and conferences—how do they help us assess our students?

Student-composed sticky and other notes written during interactive read-alouds and shared reading can be collected. They provide written evidence of an individual's or a group's thinking. How students undertook the task allows you to make decisions on the next lesson, the next text, and how much responsibility to release to students. Releasing responsibility is tricky, and this ongoing feedback must be used to make the decision. When we release students too early, they will not be able to apply the strategy independently, though it is not difficult to back up and provide more support for students. However, if we scaffold students for too long, they will not become responsible for their own learning. They will lack a sense of ownership of the thinking, which is needed for independence.

Students recording their thinking on sticky notes.

In Val's first interactive read-aloud about the moon in Chapter 5, she asked students to bring sticky notes and colored pencils to the meeting area. They recorded what they knew about the moon and added the new information they gained as Val read the book.

A quick review of these notes showed Val that most of her students were able to add new ideas to their notes, but one student's clearly showed some confusion. Val then knew that most students were ready for the next step but that she would need to confer with this student before or during the next lesson.

Reading conferences are a natural extension of interactive read-alouds and shared reading lessons. These individual conversations between student and teacher allow information to flow between both at a level appropriate for each student. The text used for the conference is usually a text the student has chosen for independent reading. Conferences are the part of the cycle of feedback, instruction, and assessment that is essential to "good first teaching." Of course, none of us can do them as frequently as we would like, but a plan for ongoing conferences is essential to make whole-group lessons as productive as possible.

Parting Thoughts . . .

"Why wait until the end of reading to assess, when listening, observing and asking questions along the way will give us so much information about our readers and inform our instruction?"

—Franki Sibberson and Karen Szymusiak (2008, p. 18)

Assessment of comprehension by individual students is at the cutting edge of our craft as teachers. Many of us have responsibilities for classes of 25 students or more. If we don't find out how our students are able to think about texts with meaningful comprehension, we cannot be sure of moving them forward. The assessment we are talking about here is "on the run" and taken during the teaching interactions. Paper-and-pen notes collected from students play a part, but question-and-answer worksheets completed by students is not enough to move our teaching from the merely literal or surface structures to the deeper structures on which all proficient readers rely.

While we use information from responses that students give during interactive read-aloud and shared reading to plan instruction, assessment of individual students is conducted in other parts of their reading instruction. Conference notes, anecdotal notes taken during small-group instruction, running records on familiar and unfamiliar texts, and benchmark assessments give both a formative and summative assessment of each student. As teachers, we need to use all our assessments to map out a plan for instruction for the whole class as well as small groups and individual students.

Professional References Cited

Bluestein, N. A. (2010). Unlocking text features for determining importance in expository text: A strategy for struggling readers. *The Reading Teacher, 63*(7), 597–600.

Duke. N. K. (1999). *Using nonfiction to increase reading achievement and word knowledge.* Occasional paper of the Scholastic Center for Literacy and Learning, New York.

Harvey, S., & Daniels, H. (2009). *Comprehension and collaboration.* Portsmouth, NH: Heinemann.

Harvey, S., & Goudvis, A. (2000). *Strategies that work: Teaching comprehension to enhance understanding.* Portland, ME: Stenhouse.

Hoyt, L., Mooney, M., & Parkes, B. (Eds.). (2003). *Exploring informational texts: From theory to practice.* Portsmouth, NH: Heinemann.

Keene, E. O. (2008). *To understand: New horizons in reading comprehension.* Portsmouth, NH: Heinemann.

Routman, R. (2002). *Reading essentials: The specifics you need to teach reading well.* Portsmouth, NH: Heinemann.

Routman, R. (2008). *Teaching essentials: Expecting the most and getting the best from every learner, K–8.* Portsmouth, NH: Heinemann.

Sibberson, F., & Szymusiak, K. (2008). *Day-to-day assessment in the reading workshop: Making informed instructional decisions in grades 3–6.* New York: Scholastic.

Tang, R. (2006). Helping students to see "genres" as more than "text types." *The Internet TESL Journal, 12*(8). Retrieved March 19, 2009 from http://iteslj.org/Techniques/Tang-Genres.

Vygotsky, L. S. (1978). *Mind in society: The development of higher psychological processes.* Cambridge, MA: Harvard University Press.

Wiggins, G., & McTighe, J. (2006). *Understanding by design.* (2nd ed.). Englewood Cliffs, NJ: Prentice Hall.

Wilhelm, J. D. (2001). *Improving comprehension with think-aloud strategies.* New York: Scholastic.

Wilhelm, J. D. (2007). *Engaging readers & writers with inquiry: Promoting deep understandings in language arts and the content areas with guiding questions.* New York: Scholastic.

Children's Literature Cited

Applegate, R. (2009). *Roscoe Riley rules #6: Never walk in shoes that talk*. New York: HarperCollins.

Bagert, B. (2005). *Giant children*. New York: Puffin.

Bradby, M. (1995). *More than anything else*. New York: Scholastic.

Brisson, P. (1999). *The summer my father was ten*. Honesdale, PA: Boyds Mills Press.

Browne, A. (1998). *Voices in the park*. New York: DK Publishing.

David, L., & Gordon, C. (2008). *Get down to Earth! What you can do to stop global warming*. New York: Scholastic.

Davies, N. (2001). *Big blue whale*. Cambridge, MA: Candlewick.

Davies, N. (2004). *Bat loves the night*. Cambridge, MA: Candlewick.

Davies, N. (2005a). *One tiny turtle*. Cambridge, MA: Candlewick.

Davies, N. (2005b). *Surprising sharks*. Cambridge, MA: Candlewick.

Friedman, R. (2008). *The silent witness: A true story of the Civil War*. San Anselmo, CA: Sandpiper.

George, J. C. (2009). *The last polar bear*. New York: HarperCollins.

Graham, P. (1999). *Speaking of journals*. Honesdale, PA: Boyds Mills Press.

Greenberg, J. C. (2002). *Andrew lost on the dog*. New York: Random House.

Hawas, Z. (2005). "King Tut: Modern science comes face-to-face with an ancient mystery." *National Geographic Explorer, 5(1)*, 10.

He waits on his porch for his teacher to pick him up. (2005, February 27). Retrieved from http://pratie.blogspot.com/2005/02/he-waits-on-his-porch-for-his teacher.html.

Henkes, K. (1996). *Chrysanthemum*. New York: HarperTrophy.

Hest, A. (2007). *Mr. George Baker*. Cambridge, MA: Candlewick.

Howker, J. (2002). *Walk with a wolf*. Cambridge, MA: Candlewick.

Jenkins, M. (2002). *The emperor's egg*. Cambridge, MA: Candlewick.

Johnston, T. (2008). *The harmonica*. Watertown, MA: Charlesbridge.

Kroll, V. (2005). *Equal shmequal: A math adventure*. Watertown, MA: Charlesbridge.

Levine, E. (2007). *Henry's freedom box*. New York: Scholastic.

Lin, G., & McKneally, R. (2006). *Our seasons*. Watertown, MA: Charlesbridge.

Lyon, G. E. (2009). *You and me and home sweet home*. New York: Atheneum.

Masoff, J. (2000). *Oh, yuck! The encyclopedia of everything nasty*. New York: Workman Publishing.

McNulty, F. (2005). *If you decide to go to the moon*. New York: Scholastic.

Pfeffer, W. (2006). *We gather together: Celebrating the harvest season.* New York: Dutton Children's Books.

Polacco, P. (1994). *Pink and Say.* New York: Philomel.

Polacco, P. (2001). *Thank you, Mr. Falker.* New York, Scholastic.

Rael, E. (2001). *Rivka's first Thanksgiving.* New York: Aladdin.

Ransom, C. F. (2002). *The promise quilt.* New York: Walker and Co.

Science News for Kids. (2009, October 7). Not bone-dry after all: The moon holds water. Retrieved from http://www.sciencenewsfor kids.org/articles/20091007/Feature1.asp.

Simon, S. (2005). *Amazing bats.* San Francisco: Chronicle Books.

Simon, S. (2002). *Killer whales.* San Francisco: Chronicle Books.

Simon, S. (2006). *Volcanoes.* San Francisco: HarperCollins.

Skurzynski, G. (2009). Home sweet moon. *ASK, 8*(2), 16–23.

Teague, M. (2002). *Dear Mrs. LaRue: Letters from obedience school.* New York: Scholastic.

Thomas, M., & Cerf, C. (Eds.). (2004). *Thanks and giving all year long.* New York: Simon & Schuster.

Trivizas, E. (1997). *The three little wolves and the big bad pig.* New York: McElderry.

Tsuchiya, Y. (1997). *Faithful elephants: A true story of animals, people, and war.* San Anselmo, CA: Sandpiper.

Waber, B. (1994). *But names will never hurt me.* San Anselmo, CA: Sandpiper.

Wiles, D. (2001). *Freedom summer.* New York: Aladdin.

Woodson, J. (2006). *Hush.* New York: G. P. Putnam's Sons.

Appendix

COMPREHENSION STRATEGIES TERMINOLOGY CHART

Ellin Keene *New Horizons*	Harvey and Goudvis *Strategies That Work*	Debbie Miller *Reading With Meaning*	Fountas and Pinnell *Continuum of Literacy*
Relating new to known (Schema)	Making Connections	Schema	Making Connections
Determining Importance	Determining Importance	Digging Deeper	
Evoking Images	Visualizing	Creating Mental Images	
Questioning	Questioning	Asking Questions	
Inferring	Inferring	Inferring	Inferring
Synthesizing	Synthesizing Retelling	Synthesizing	Synthesizing
Monitoring for Meaning			
			Analyzing
			Critiquing
			Predicting

Monitoring for Meaning

Bradby, M. (1995). *More than anything else.* New York: Scholastic.

Browne, A. (1998). *Voices in the park.* New York: DK Publishing.

Cooper, M. (1997). *I got a family.* New York: Henry Holt.

Crelin, B. (2004). *There once was a sky full of stars.* Cambridge, MA: Sky Publishing.

Jenkins, M. (2002). *The emperor's egg.* Cambridge, MA: Candlewick Press.

Keller, L. (2002). *The scrambled states of America.* New York: Henry Holt.

Kroll, V. (2009). *Selvakumar knew better.* Walnut Creek, CA: Shen's Books.

Lin, G. (2009). *The ugly vegetables.* Watertown, MA: Charlesbridge Publishing.

Noble, T. H. (2004). *The scarlet stockings spy.* Chelsea, MI: Sleeping Bear Press.

Priceman, M. (2005). *Hot air: The (mostly) true story of the first hot-air balloon ride.*
    New York: Atheneum.

Teague, M. (2002). *Dear Mrs. LaRue: Letters from obedience school.* New York: Scholastic.

Determining Importance

Adkins, J. (2006). *What if you met a pirate?* Milford, CT: Roaring Brook Press.

Bailey, J. (2006). *Cracking up: A story about erosion.* Minneapolis, MN: Picture Window Books.

Collard, S. B., III. (1998). *Animal dazzlers: The role of brilliant colors in nature.* New York:
    Franklin Watts.

Lasky, K. (2003). *Vision of beauty: The story of Sarah Breedlove Walker.* Cambridge, MA:
    Candlewick.

Lin, G. & McNeally, R. (2006). *Our seasons.* Watertown, MA: Charlesbridge.

Pfeffer, W. (2006). *We gather together.* New York: Dutton Children's Books.

Rylant, C. (1982). *When I was young in the mountains.* New York: Dutton Children's Books.

Creating Mental Images

Borden, L. (2005). *America is . . .* New York: Aladdin.

Bunting, E. (1994). *Night of the gargoyles.* New York: Clarion.

Elliott, D. (2009). *And here's to you!* Cambridge, MA: Candlewick.

Fletcher, R. (1997). *Twilight comes twice.* New York: Clarion.

Greenberg, J. C. (2002). *Andrew lost on the dog.* New York: Random House.

Guiberson, B. (2010). *Moon bear.* New York: Scholastic.

Jenkins, S., & Page, R. (2003). *What do you do with a tail like this?* Boston: Houghton Mifflin.

Lewis, J. P. (2001). *A burst of firsts: Doers, shakers, and record breakers.* New York: Dial.

Locker, T. (2001). *Mountain dance.* Cambridge, MA: Candlewick.

London, J. (1999). *Condor's egg.* San Francisco: Chronicle.

Noda, T. (2003). *Dear world.* New York: Dial Books for Young Readers.

Pilkey, D. (1999). *The paperboy.* New York: Scholastic.

Rylant, C. (1991). *Night in the country.* New York: Aladdin.

Thompson, S. L. (2005). *Imagine a day.* New York: Atheneum.

Wild, M. (1994). *Our granny.* Boston: Houghton Mifflin.

Wood, D. (2010). *Where the sunrise begins.* New York: Simon & Schuster.

Yolen, J. (2003). *Color me a rhyme.* Honesdale, PA: Boyds Mills Press.

Inferring

Bloom, S. (2005). *A splendid friend, indeed.* Honesdale, PA: Boyds Mills Press.

Browne, A. (1990). *Changes.* New York: Farrar, Straus & Giroux.

Brumbeau, J. (2002). *The quiltmaker's gift.* New York: Scholastic.

Bunting, E. (1991). *Night tree.* New York: Voyager Books.

Cohen, M. (2005). *My big brother.* New York: Star Bright Books.

Coyle, C. L. (2006). *Thank you, Aunt Tallulah!* Lanham, MD: Rising Moon Books.

Fox, M. (1992). *Hattie and the fox.* New York: Aladdin.

Hest, A. (2004). *Mr. George Baker.* Cambridge, MA: Candlewick.

Mobin-Uddin, A. (2005). *My name is Bilal.* Honesdale, PA: Boyds Mills Press.

Polacco, P. (1995). *Babushka's doll.* New York: Aladdin.

Spinelli, E. (1996). *Somebody loves you, Mr. Hatch.* New York: Simon & Schuster.

Trivizas, E. (1997). *The three little wolves and the big bad pig.* New York: McElderry.

Willems, M. (2010). *City dog, country frog.* New York: Hyperion.

Williams, L. E. (2006). *The best winds.* Honesdale, PA: Boyds Mills Press.

Schema/Making Connections

Blabey, A. (2008). *Sunday chutney.* Honesdale, PA: Boyds Mill Press.

Brisson, P. (1999). *The summer my father was ten.* Honesdale, PA: Boyds Mills Press.

Catrow, D. (2002). *We the kids: The preamble to the Constitution of the United States.* New York: Puffin.

Collard, S. B., III. (2002). *Leaving home.* Boston: Houghton Mifflin.

Fleming, C. (2005). *Sunny boy!* The life and times of a tortoise. New York: Farrar, Straus & Giroux.

Gerritsen, P. (2006). *Nuts.* Asheville, NC: Front Street Books.

Kelly, I. (2005). *A small dog's big life: Around the world with Owney.* New York: Holiday House.

Lichtenheld, T. (2007). *What are you so grumpy about?* New York: Little, Brown.

Levine, E. (2007). *Henry's freedom box.* New York: Scholastic.

Llewellyn, B. M. (2009). *One child, one planet.* Auburn Hills, MI: Emerald Shamrock Press.

McKay, L., Jr. (2000). *Journey home.* New York: Lee & Low Books.

Penner, L. R. (2002). *Liberty! How the Revolutionary War began.* New York: Random House.

Simon, S. (2002). *Killer whales.* San Francisco: Chronicle Books.

Simon, S. (2005). *Amazing bats.* San Francisco: Chronicle Books.

Tsuchiya, Y. (1997). *Faithful elephants: A true story of animals, people, and war.* San Anselmo, CA: Sandpiper.

Wells, R. (2001). *Yoko's paper cranes.* New York: Hyperion.

Asking Questions

Abercrombie, B. (1995). *Charlie Anderson.* New York: Aladdin.

Bunting, E. (1998). *The Wednesday surprise.* San Anselmo, CA: Sandpiper.

Bunting, E. (1993). *Fly away home.* San Anselmo, CA: Sandpiper.

Cox, J. (1998). *Now we can have a wedding!* New York: Holiday House.

Deedy, C. A. (2009). *14 cows for America.* Atlanta: Peachtree Publishers.

Forman, M. (1997). *From wax to crayon.* Danbury, CT: Children's Press.

Frasier, D. (2007). *Miss Alaineus: A vocabulary disaster.* San Anselmo, CA: Sandpiper.

Gaiman, N. (2006). *The day I swapped my dad for two goldfish.* New York: HarperCollins.

Larson, K., & Nethery, M. (2008). *Two Bobbies: The true story of Hurricane Katrina, friendship, and survival.* New York: Walker and Co.

Lasky, K. (1994). *The librarian who measured the Earth.* New York: Little, Brown.

Lyon, G. E. (2009). *You and me and home sweet home.* New York: Atheneum.

Mochizuki, K. (1995). *Heroes.* New York: Lee & Low.

Mochizuki, K. (2003). *Passage to freedom.* New York: Lee & Low Books.

Rael, E. (2001). *Rivka's first Thanksgiving.* New York: Aladdin.

Woodson, J. (2001). *The other side.* New York: G. P. Putnam's Sons.

Synthesis

Coles, R. (2004). *The story of Ruby Bridges.* New York: Scholastic.

French, J. (2009). *Diary of a wombat.* New York: Clarion.

Hatkoff, J., Hatkoff, I., & Hatkoff, C. (2009). *Winter's tail: How one little dolphin learned to swim again.* New York: Scholastic.

Hatkoff, I., Hatkoff, C., & Kahumba, P. (2006). *Owen and Mzee: The true story of a remarkable friendship.* New York: Scholastic.

Howker, J. (2002). *Walk with a wolf.* Cambridge, MA: Candlewick.

Lowell, S. (2000). *Cindy Ellen: A wild western Cinderella.* New York: HarperCollins.

Mortenson, G., & Roth, S. (2009). *Listen to the wind: The story of Dr. Greg and Three Cups of Tea.* New York: Dial Books for Young Readers.

Muth, J. (2002). *The three questions (based on a story by Leo Tolstoy).* New York: Scholastic.

Pallotta, J. (2004). *Dory story.* Watertown, MA: Charlesbridge.

Rylant, C. (1996). *The old woman who named things.* New York: Harcourt.

Say, A. (1999). *Tea with milk.* Boston: Houghton Mifflin.

Willems, M. (2004). *Don't let the pigeon drive the bus!* New York: Scholastic.

Willems, M. (2009). *Naked mole rat gets dressed.* New York: Hyperion.

Winter, J. (2008). *Wangari's trees of peace: A true story from Africa.* Cambridge, MA: Candlewick.

Text Types

Simple informational

Bernard, R. (1999). *A tree for all seasons.* New York: National Geographic Children's Books.

De Capua, S. (2003). *New York.* Danbury, CT: Children's Press. (There are many titles in the Rookie Read-About Geography series.)

Dussling, J. (1998). *Bugs! Bugs! Bugs!* New York: DK Publishing.

Gilbert, S. (2010). *Dump trucks (Machines That Build).* Ontario, Canada: Saunders.

Iasevoli, B. & the editors of *Time for Kids.* (2006). *Plants!* New York: Harper Collins. (This is a book at the lowest level of the Science Scoops series. There are more books at this level, and there are two more levels.)

Schuette, S. (2005). *Mountain biking.* Mankato, MI: Capstone Press.

Stewart, M. (2006). *Energy in motion.* New York: Scholastic. (There are many titles in the Rookie Read-About Science series.)

Fairy Tales

Brett, J. (1992). *Goldilocks and the three bears.* New York: Putnam Juvenile.

Coburn, J. (2000). *Domitila: A Cinderella tale from the Mexican tradition.* Walnut Creek, CA: Shen's Books.

Craft, M. F. (2002). *Sleeping Beauty.* San Francisco: Chronicle Books.

Galdone, P. (1974). *Little red riding hood.* New York: McGraw-Hill. (Galdone has retold many traditional fairy tales.)

Hale, B. (2008). *Snoring beauty.* New York: Harcourt.

Kellogg, S. (1997). *Jack and the beanstalk.* New York: HarperCollins. (Steven Kellogg has also written *Chicken Little.*)

Marshall, J. (2000). *The three little pigs.* New York: Grosset & Dunlap. (James Marshall has retold "Goldilocks and the Three Bears," "Little Red Riding Hood," "Cinderella," and "Hansel and Gretel.")

Muth, J. (2003). *Stone soup.* New York: Scholastic.

Roberts, L. (2003). *Rapunzel: A groovy fairy tale.* New York: Abrams.

Scieszka, J. (1998). *The stinky cheese man and other fairly stupid tales.* New York: Puffin.

Tucker, K. (2003). *The seven Chinese sisters.* New York: Albert Whitman and Co.

Poetry

Andrews, J., & Hamilton, E. W. (2009). *Julie Andrews' collection of poems, songs, and lullabies.* New York: Little, Brown.

Bagert, B. (2005). *Giant children.* New York: Puffin.

Florian, D. (1998). *Beast feast.* New York: Voyager Books.

Florian, D. (2007). *Comets, stars, the moon, and Mars.* New York: Harcourt.

Giovanni, N. (Ed.). (2008). *Hip hop speaks to children: A celebration of poetry with a beat.* Naperville, IL: Sourcebooks.

Katz, A. (2010). *Too much kissing! And other silly dilly songs about parents.* New York: Simon & Schuster.

Kennedy, C. (Ed.). (2005). *A family of poems: My favorite poetry for children.* New York: Hyperion.

Paschen, E. (Ed.). (2005). *Poetry speaks to children.* Naperville IL: Sourcebooks.

San José, C., & Johnson, B. (Eds.) (2009). *Every second something happens,* Honesdale, PA: Wordsong.

Singer, M. (2008). *First food fight this fall and other school poems.* New York: Sterling.

Smith, C. R., Jr. (2000). *Rimshots.* New York: Puffin.

Smith, C. R., Jr. (2007). *Hoop kings.* Cambridge, MA: Candlewick.

Smith, C. R., Jr. (2007). *Hoop queens.* Cambridge, MA: Candlewick.

Realistic Fiction

Brinckloe, J. (1986). *Fireflies.* New York: Aladdin.

Bunting, E. (1994). *A day's work.* New York: Clarion.

Bunting, E. (2001). *Gleam and Glow.* New York: Harcourt.

dePaolo, T. (2000). *Nana upstairs and Nana downstairs.* New York: Puffin.

Isadora, R. (1994). *The crossroads.* New York: Greenwillow.

Javaherbin, M. (2010). *Goal!* Cambridge, MA: Candlewick.

McBrier, P. (2004). *Beatrice's goat.* New York: Aladdin.

Martin, B., Jr., & Archambault, J. (1997). *Knots on a counting rope.* New York: Henry Holt.

Polacco, P. (1993). *Mrs. Katz and Tush.* New York: Bantam.

Polacco, P. (2007). *The lemonade club.* New York: Philomel Books.

Say, A. (2003). *Emma's rug.* New York: Harcourt.

Williams, V. B. (1984). *A chair for my mother.* New York: Greenwillow.

Biography

Bryant, J. (2008). *A river of words: The story of William Carlos Williams.* Grand Rapids, MI:
    Eerdmans Books for Young Readers.

Giblin, J. C. (2007). *The many rides of Paul Revere.* New York: Scholastic.

Krull, K. (2004). *A woman for president: The story of Victoria Woodhull.* New York:
    Walker and Company.

Krull, K. (2010). *The brothers Kennedy: John, Robert, Edward.* New York: Simon & Schuster.

Rappaport, D. (2009). *Eleanor, quiet no more.* New York: Hyperion.

Rockwell, A. (2009). *Big George: How a shy boy became President Washington.*
    New York: Harcourt.

Venezia, M. (2009). *Mary Leakey: Archaeologist who really dug her work.* New York: Scholastic.
    (This is one book is a series of biographies from Scholastic.)

Wade, M. D. (2009). *David Crockett: Creating a legend.* Houston: Bright Sky Press.

Wallner, A. (2001). *Abigail Adams.* New York: Holiday House.

Yolen, J. (2010). *All star! Honus Wagner and the most famous baseball card ever.*
    New York: Penguin.

Mystery

Biedrzycki, D. (2005). *Ace Lacewing, bug detective.* Watertown, MA: Charlesbridge Publishing.

Christelow, E. (1986). *The robbery at the Diamond Dog Diner.* New York: Clarion.

Clement, R. (1999). *Grandpa's teeth.* New York: HarperCollins.

Kitamura, S. (1996). *Sheep in wolves' clothing.* New York: Farrar, Straus & Giroux.

Supraner, R. (1996). *Sam Sunday and the mystery at the Ocean Beach Hotel.* New York: Viking.

Teague, M. (2004). *Detective LaRue: Letters from the investigation.* New York: Scholastic.

Yolen, J. (1989). *Piggins.* New York: Harcourt.

Yolen, J. (1993). *Picnic with Piggins.* New York: Harcourt.

Literary Nonfiction

Allen, J. (2003). *Are you a spider?* Boston: Kingfisher. (Other books in this Backyard Books
    series are *Are You a Bee?, Are You a Butterfly?* and *Are You a Ladybug?*)

George, M., & Murphy, C. J. (2006). *Lucille lost: A true adventure.* New York: Penguin.

Davies, N. (2001). *Big blue whale.* Cambridge, MA: Candlewick.

Davies, N. (2004). *Bat loves the night*. Cambridge, MA: Candlewick.

Davies, N. (2005). *One tiny turtle*. Cambridge, MA: Candlewick.

Davies, N. (2005). *Surprising sharks*. Cambridge, MA: Candlewick.

Hansard, P. (2001). *A field full of horses*. Cambridge, MA: Candlewick.

Jenkins, M. (2001). *Chameleons are cool*. Cambridge, MA: Candlewick.

King-Smith, D. (2001). *All pigs are beautiful*. Cambridge, MA: Candlewick.

Historical Fiction

Bildner, P. (2010). *The hallelujah flight*. Toronto: Putnam Juvenile.

Birtha, B. (2005). *Grandmama's pride*. Park Ridge, IL: Albert Whitman & Co.

Friddell, C. (2010). *Goliath: Hero of the great Baltimore fire*. Ann Arbor, MI:
Sleeping Bear Press.

Friedman, R. (2008). *The silent witness: A true story of the Civil War*. Boston: Houghton Mifflin.

Gray, L. M. (1993). *Dear Willie Rudd*. New York: Aladdin.

Johnson, A. (2004). *Just like Josh Gibson*. New York: Simon & Schuster.

Johnston, T. (2008). *The harmonica*. Watertown, MA: Charlesbridge.

Miller, W. (1999). *Richard Wright and the library card*. New York: Lee & Low.

Mochizuki, K. (1993). *Baseball saved us*. New York: Lee & Low.

Robinson, S. (2009). *Testing the ice: A true story about Jackie Robinson*. New York: Scholastic.

Wiles, D. (2001). *Freedom summer*. New York: Aladdin.

Graphic Novels

Cammuso, F. (2008). *Knights of the lunch table: The dodgeball chronicles*. New York: Scholastic.

Craddock, E. (2009). *BC Mambo*. New York: Random House.

Doeden, M. (2006). *Winter at Valley Forge*. Mankato, MN: Capstone. (This is part of the
Graphic Library series, which includes Graphic History titles and Graphic
Biographies titles.)

Meister, C. (2010). *Clues in the attic (My First Graphic Novel)*. Mankato, MN: Capstone.

Powell, M. (2010). *The tall tale of Paul Bunyan*. Mankato, MN: Capstone.
(This is one in a series.)

Spires, A. (2009). *Binky the Space Cat*. Toronto: Kids Can Press.

Science Fiction

Breathed, B. (2007). *Mars needs moms!* New York: Philomel.

Brett, J. (2006). *Hedgie blasts off!* New York: Penguin.

Gall, C. (2008). *There's nothing to do on Mars.* New York: Little, Brown.

Marshall, E. (1992). *Space case.* New York: Puffin.

O'Malley, K., & O'Brien, P. (2007). *Captain Raptor and the space pirates.* New York: Walker and Co.

Fantasy

Franson, S. (2007). *Un-Brella.* Milford, CT: Roaring Brook Press.

Gall, C. (2006). *Dear fish.* New York: Little, Brown.

Pawagi, M. (2010). *The girl who hated books.* Toronto: Second Story Press.

Rohmann, E. (2005). *Clara and Asha.* Milford, CT: Roaring Brook Press.

Rymond, L. G. (2007). *Oscar and the mooncats.* Boston: Houghton Mifflin.

Say, A. (1988). *A river dream.* Boston: Houghton Mifflin.

Hybrid Texts (texts with more than one genre)

Halls, K. M. (2010). *Saving the Baghdad zoo: A true story of hope and heroes.* New York: Greenwillow.

Jenkins, S. (1999). *The top of the world: Climbing Mount Everest.* Boston: Houghton Mifflin.

Kitchen, B. (1994). *Somewhere today.* Cambridge, MA: Candlewick.

Mortenson, G., & Roth, S. (2009). *Listen to the wind: The story of Dr. Greg and Three Cups of Tea.* New York: Dial Books for Young Readers.

Stewart, D. (2007). *You wouldn't want to sail on the Titanic!* New York: Scholastic.

Sylver, A. (2010). *Hot diggity dog: The history of the hot dog.* New York: Dutton.

Weigel, J. (2010). *Thunder from the sea: The adventures of Jack Hoyton and the HMS Defender.* New York: Putnam.

Text Structures

Cause and Effect

Aardema, V. (1980). *Why mosquitoes buzz in people's ears.* New York: Scholastic.

Branley, F. M. (1985). *What makes day and night.* New York: Harper & Row.

David, L., & Gordon, C. (2008). *Get down to Earth! What you can do to stop global warming.* New York: Scholastic.

Heller, R. (1983). *The reason for a flower.* New York: Grosset & Dunlap.

Jenkins, S. (2009). *Never smile at a monkey: And 17 other important things to remember.* New York: Houghton Mifflin.

Jenkins, S., & Page, R. (2010). *How to clean a hippopotamus: A look at unusual animal partnerships.* New York: Houghton Mifflin.

Rath, T., & Reckmeyer, M. (2009). *How full is your bucket? For kids.* New York: Gallup.

Turner, A. (1995). *Nettie's trip south.* New York: Aladdin.

Problem and Solution

Arnosky, J. (2010). *Slow down for manatees.* Toronto, Canada: Putnam.

George, J. C. (2010). *The buffalo are back.* New York: Dutton.

Goodall, J. (2004). *Rickie and Henri: A true story.* New York: Minedition.

Jackson, D. (2000). *The wildlife detectives: How forensic scientists fight crimes against nature.* New York: Houghton Mifflin.

Napoli, D. (2010). *Mama Miti.* New York: Simon & Schuster.

Rotner, S. & Woodhull, A. (2010). *The buzz on bees: Why are they disappearing?* New York: Holiday House.

Chronological, Sequence, or Time Order

Cronin, D. (2004). *Diary of a worm.* New York: Scholastic.

Cronin, D. (2005). *Diary of a spider.* New York. HarperCollins.

de Fatima Campos, M. (2010). *Cássio's day: From dawn to dusk in a Brazilian village (A child's day).* London: Frances Lincoln Children's Books. (This series contains more books about other countries.)

Eubank, P. R. (2010). *Seaman's journey: On the trail with Lewis and Clark.* Nashville, TN: Ideals Children's Books.

Heiligman, D. (1996). *From caterpillar to butterfly.* New York: HarperCollins.

Millard, A. (1998). *A street through time.* New York: DK Publishing.

Provensen, A. (1990). *The buck stops here: The presidents of the United States.* New York: HarperCollins.

Spradlin, M. (2010). *Off like the wind! The first ride of the Pony Express.* New York: Walker.

Yolen, J. (2008). *Naming liberty.* New York: Penguin.

Description

Branley, F. M. (1986). *What the moon is like.* New York: Harper & Row.

Jenkins, S. (2007). *Living color.* New York: Houghton Mifflin.

Resnick, J. P. (2010). *Sharks* (Photo-fact collection series). Chicago: Kidsbooks. (This series includes *Insects, Snakes, Reptiles, Horses, Spiders, Whales and Dolphins,* and *Dogs.*)

Compare and Contrast

Fandangleman, R. (2009). *Comparing creatures.* Chicago: Heinemann-Raintree.

Hillman, B. (2007). *How big is it?* New York: Scholastic.

Jenkins, S. (2004). *Actual size.* Boston: Houghton Mifflin.

Question and Answer

Allen, P. (1988). *Who sank the boat?* New York: Puffin.

Avison, B. (1997). *I wonder why I blink and other questions about my body.* Boston: Kingfisher.

Laffon, M. (2010). *The book of why.* New York: Macmillan. (This series includes *The Book of What, The Book of How,* and *The Book of Who.*)

Orme, H. (2009). *Seeds, bulbs, plants and flowers.* Tunbridge Wells, Kent, UK: TickTock Books.

Prap, L. (2005). *Why?* La Jolla, CA: Kane/Miller Book Publishers.

Seuling, B. (1998). *Winter lullaby.* New York: Voyager Books.

Smith, D. (2009). *If America were a village: A book about the people of the United States.* Toronto: Kids Can Press.

Theodorou, R. (2001). *Black rhino (Animals in danger).* Chicago, IL: Heinemann Library.

Enumeration

Brunelle, L. (2007). *Camp out! The ultimate kids' guide*. New York: Workman.

Carney, M. (2005). *Bird-watching*. Harlow, Essex, UK: DK Celebration Press/
Pearson Learning.

Pearson, D. (2005). *Make it, wear it*. Harlow, Essex, UK: DK Celebration Press/
Pearson Learning.

Russell, T. (1997). *Magic step-by-step*. New York: Sterling.

Text Features

Bailey, J. (2002). *Bug Dictionary: An A to Z of insects and creepy crawlies*. New York: Scholastic.

DK Eye Wonder. (2004). *Rocks and minerals*. New York: DK Publishing.

DK Eyewitness Books. (2009). *Titanic*. New York: DK Publishing.

Gibbons, G. (1995). *Sea turtles*. New York: Holiday House. (Gail Gibbons has written many
nonfiction picture books that contain a variety of text features.)

Jenkins, S., & Page, R. (2003). *What do you do with a tail like this?* Boston: Houghton Mifflin.
(Steve Jenkins has written many nonfiction picture books that contain a variety of
text features.)

Mugford, S. (2005). *Sharks and other dangers of the deep*. New York: St. Martin's Press.

Murphy, G. (2008). *A kid's guide to global warming*. Sydney: Weldon Owen.

Salzano, T. (2008). *Poison*. New York: Scholastic.

Showers, P. (1994). *Where does the garbage go?* New York: HarperCollins.

Content Area

Social Studies

Cook, P. (2006). *You wouldn't want to be at the Boston Tea Party! Wharf water tea you'd rather not
drink*. New York: Franklin Watts. (This series includes *You Wouldn't Want to Be an
American Colonist!: A Settlement You'd Rather Not Start, You Wouldn't Want to Be an American
Pioneer! A Wilderness You'd Rather Not Tame, You Wouldn't Want to Be in a Medieval Dungeon!
Prisoners You'd Rather Not Meet, You Wouldn't Want to Be an Egyptian Mummy! Disgusting
Things You'd Rather Not Know, You Wouldn't Want to Sail With Christopher Columbus!
Uncharted Waters You'd Rather Not Cross, You Wouldn't Want to Sail on the Mayflower! A Trip
That Took Entirely Too Long.*)

DK Eyewitness Books. *Presidents*. New York: DK Publishing.

Levine, E. (2007). *Henry's freedom box.* New York: Scholastic.

Maestro, B., & Maestro, G. (1987). *A more perfect union.* New York: HarperCollins.

Rozett, L. (Ed.). (2010). *Fast facts about the 50 states.* New York: Scholastic.

Shore, D. Z., & Alexander, J. (2006). *This is the dream.* New York: HarperCollins.

Talbott, H. (2009). *River of dreams: The story of the Hudson River.* New York: Penguin.

Tunnell, M. (1997). *Mailing May.* New York: Greenwillow.

Science and Math

Branley, F. M., *Volcanoes.* New York: HarperTrophy. (Stage 2 Let's-Read-And-Find-Out Science series includes books on the human body, plants and animals, dinosaurs, outer space, weather and the seasons, and Earth.)

Hutchins, P. (1989). *The doorbell rang.* New York: Greenwillow.

Kroll, V. (2005). *Equal shmequal: A math adventure.* Watertown, MA: Charlesbridge.

Lewis, J. P. (2002). *Arithme-Tickle.* New York: Harcourt.

Locker, T. (2000). *Cloud dance.* New York: Harcourt.

McNulty, F. (2005). *If you decide to go to the moon.* New York: Scholastic.

Nagda, A. W. (2002). *Tiger math.* New York: Owlet Paperbacks.

Pinczes, E. (1995). *A remainder of one.* Boston: Houghton Mifflin.

Tang, G. (2001). *The grapes of math.* New York: Scholastic.

Tang, G. (2003). *Math-terpieces: The art of problem-solving.* New York: Scholastic.

Tang, G. (2005). *Math potatoes.* New York: Scholastic.

Resources for Shared Reading

Bateman, T. (2001). *Red, white, blue, and Uncle Who? The stories behind some of America's patriotic symbols.* New York: Holiday House.

Bolden, T. (2003). *Portraits of African-American heroes.* New York: Scholastic.

Canfield, J. (1998). *Chicken soup for the kid's soul.* Deerfield Beach, FL: Health Communications.

Farndon, J. (2004). *The big book of knowledge.* Bath, UK: Parragon.

Masoff, J. (2000). *Oh, yuck! The encyclopedia of everything nasty.* New York: Workman Publishing.

Masoff, J. (2006). *Oh, yikes! History's grossest, wackiest moments.* New York: Workman.

Simonds, N., Swartz, L., & The Children's Museum, Boston. (2002). *Moonbeams, dumplings and dragon boats.* Orlando, FL: Harcourt.

Tesar, J., & Glassman, B. (2004). *Kidbits: More than 1,500 eye-popping charts, graphs, maps and visuals that instantly show you everything you want to know about your world!* Farmington Hills, MI: Blackbirch Press.

Thimmesh, C. (2002). *Girls think of everything: Stories of ingenious inventions by women.* Boston: Houghton Mifflin.

Thomas, M., and Cerf, C. (Eds.). (2004). *Thanks and giving: All year long.* New York: Simon & Schuster.

Almanacs

The Old Farmer's Almanac for Kids. Dublin, NH: Yankee.

Time For Kids. New York: Time Inc.

The World Almanac for Kids. New York: World Almanac Books.

Big Books

Mondo Bookshop. New York: Mondo Publishing.

National Geographic: Windows on Literacy. Washington, D.C.: National Geographic Society.

Newbridge Big Books. Northborough, MA: Newbridge Educational.

Rigby Literacy. Barrington IL: Rigby.

Magazines

ASK

Boys' Life

Click

Dig

Girls' Life

National Geographic Kids

Ranger Rick

Scholastic News

Spider

Sports Illustrated for Kids

Time for Kids